A First Book in American History

A First Book in American History

History

by Edward Eggleston

©2011 SMK Books

Wilder Publications, LLC.
PO Box 3005
Radford VA 24143-3005

ISBN 10: 1-61720-392-0
ISBN 13: 978-1-61720-392-3

Table of Contents:

The Early Life of Columbus

More than four hundred years ago there lived in the old city of Genoa, in Italy, a workingman who had four sons. One of these was Christopher Columbus, who was born, probably about the year 1446, in that part of the city occupied by the weavers of woolen cloth. Learned men have lately taken much pains to find the very house. It is a narrow house, and dark inside. The city has bought it and put an inscription in Latin on the front, which says: "No house more worthy! Here, under his father's roof, Christopher Columbus passed his boyhood and youth." The father of little Christopher was a wool comber—that is, a man who prepared the wool for the spinners, or, as some say, a weaver. Christopher learned to work in wool, like his father.

At this time Genoa was a place of ships and sailors, going and coming to and from many parts of the world. On the beach he might have seen the fishermen launch their boats and spread their curious pointed sails, such as you see in the picture. From the wharves of Genoa he could watch the ships sailing out to trade in distant lands. I wonder if the wool-comber's little boy ever dreamed that he might one day come to be the most famous of all ship captains, and sail farther away into unknown seas than any man had ever sailed before.

Columbus was doubtless poor and had to work for his living. But he must have been studious, for he somehow got a pretty good education. He learned Latin, he wrote a good hand, and could draw maps and charts for the use of sailors, by which last calling he was able to support himself when he came to be a man. At twenty-four years of age Columbus made a voyage, but he was at least twenty-seven years of age when he finally became a seaman, and began to acquire that knowledge of sailing which prepared him to make discoveries. The seamen of that time did not sail very far. Their voyages were mostly in the Med-i-ter-ra'-ne-an, and they knew little of the Atlantic Ocean, which they called "The Sea of Darkness," because they did not know that was in it or on the other side of it. They believed that great monsters swam in the ocean, and that in one part it was so hot that the water boiled.

Of course, they did not know that there was any such place as America, and they believed that Africa reached clear to the south pole. The only trade they had with Asia was by caravans, which brought silks, gums, spices, and precious stones from the far East on the backs of camels.

While Columbus was yet a little boy, there was living in Portugal a prince named Henry, the son of the king of that country. Henry was a learned man, who thought he could find a way to get round Africa to the rich countries of Asia. He sent out ship after ship, until he had discovered much of the African coast.

It was probably the fame of these voyages that drew Columbus to Portugal. From Portugal Columbus himself sailed down the newly discovered coast of Africa. Then he went north beyond England, so that he was already a very great traveler for the time.

While the Portuguese, in trying to get to India, were creeping timidly down the coast of Africa, with land always in sight, Christopher Columbus conceived a new a far bolder plan. As learned man believed the world round, he proposed to sail straight west to Asia, braving all the dangers of the known Atlantic. He thought the world much smaller than it is, and he supposed that he should find Asia about as far west of Europe as America is. He did not dream of finding a new world.

As Portugal was the leading country in making discoveries, Columbus first proposed to find this new way to Asia for the king of that country. If the good Prince Henry had been alive, he would probably have adopted the plan with joy. But "Henry the Navigator," as he was called, had died long before, and the advisers of the King of Portugal ridiculed the plan, and laughed at the large reward which Columbus demanded if he should succeed. However, the king secretly sent out one of his own vessels, which sailed westward a little way, and then came back and reported that there was no land there. When Columbus heard of this, he left Portugal, not liking to be cheated in this way.

He went to Spain and appeared at court, a poor and friendless stranger. Spain was ruled at this time by King Ferdinand and Queen Isabella. They were very busy in their war with the Moors, who then occupied a great part of Spain. Columbus followed the court from place to place for years. But the king and queen paid little heed to the projects of this foreigner. They were too much employed with battles and sieges to attend to plans for finding a new way to India.

Most of those who heard of Columbus ridiculed his plans. They did not believe that people could live on the other side of the world, and walk with their feet up and their heads down. The very children tapped their foreheads when Columbus passed, to signify their belief that the fellow was crazy.

In 1491 Columbus, whose plans were at last rejected, left the court, traveling on foot like the poor man that he was, and leading his little boy by the hand. He stopped one day at the convent of La Rabida to beg a little bread and water for the child. The good prior of the convent, happening to pass at that moment, was struck with the foreign accent of the stranger's speech. He began to talk with him, and soon learned of the project that had so long filled the mind of Columbus. The prior was deeply interested. He had once been the confessor, or religious adviser, of Isabella, and he now wrote the queen a letter in favor of the plan of Columbus. The queen sent for the prior, and he persuaded her to bring back Columbus. She sent the great navigator a mule and some decent clothes.

But Columbus, when he got back to court, still demanded such high rewards if he should succeed that he was again allowed to depart. He set out to offer his plan to the King of France; but now his friends again interceded with the queen, lamenting that Spain should lose his services. The queen sent a messenger after him, who overtook him in a pass of the mountains and brought him back, with the assurance that, at last, he would be sent forth on his voyage.

How Columbus Discovered America

About two hundred years before Columbus sailed, there arrived in the city of Venice one day three travelers, coarsely dressed in Chinese fashion. They said that they were three gentlemen named Polo, who had left Venice many years before. They had almost forgotten how to speak Italian, and at first their own relatives thought them foreigners and impostors. But they gave a magnificent banquet at which they all appeared in rich robes. They changed their garments again and again as the feast went on. Every robe taken off was cut up and given to the servants. At last they took their old garments and ripped them open, and poured out before the guests a collection of precious stones of untold value.

One of these gentlemen, Marco Polo, whose portrait you see here, wrote a book of his travels, describing the vast riches of Eastern countries, before unknown to people in Europe. Columbus had read this book, and it was to find a new way to reach the rich countries seen by Polo that he was now resolved to sail partly round the globe.

In spite of the power which the King of Spain gave him to force ships and seamen to go with him, Columbus found the greatest trouble in fitting out his expedition, so much were the sailors afraid of the ocean. But at last all was ready. Those who were to sail into "The Sea of Darkness" with Columbus took the sacrament and bade a solemn farewell to their friends, feeling much like men condemned to death. They embarked in three little vessels, only one of which had a deck over it.

Columbus went to the Canary Islands first. Then with bitter lamentations the men took leave of the last known land, and sailed into seas in which no ship had ever been. Columbus tried to cheer them with the stories he had read in Marco Polo's book, of the riches of the great country of China. But he also deceived them by keeping two separate accounts of his sailing. In the one which he showed to his companions he made the distance from Spain much less than it really was.

But they were greatly alarmed to find that, as they went west, the needle of the compass did not point directly to the north star. This change, though well known now, was probably as surprising to Columbus as to his men, but he did his best to keep up their courage.

The weather was fine, and the winds blew always from the east. This alarmed the sailors more than ever, for they were sure they would get no wind to come back with. One day the wind came around to the southwest, which was a great encouragement.

But presently the ships struck great masses of seaweed, and all was grumbling and lamentation again. The frightened sailors remembered old stories of a frozen ocean, and imagined that this must be the very place. When the wind fell to a calm, they thought the ships might lie there and rot for want of wind to fill the sails.

They were getting farther and farther away from Europe. Where would they find food and water to last them till they got home? They thought their commander a crack-brained fool, who would go on to their destruction. They planned, therefore, to throw him into the sea, and go back. They could say that, while he was gazing at the stars, after his fashion, he had tumbled over.

But the worst disappointments were to come. One day the glad cry of "Land!" was raised. Columbus fell on his knees to return thanks, while the men scrambled up into the rigging. But it proved to be only a cloud. On the 7th of October another false alarm disheartened the sailors more than ever.

From the first Columbus had pointed to seaweed, and other supposed signs of land, until the men would no longer listen to his hopeful words. Now the appearance of some song birds, a heron, and a duck, could not comfort them. The great enterprise was about to end in failure, after all, when, on the 11th of October, the sailors found a branch of a thorn-tree with berries on it. At length a carved stick was found, and the men began to believe that they were really near to some inhabited land.

During the night which followed this discovery no one on the ships slept. About ten o'clock Columbus saw a glimmering light appearing and disappearing, as though someone on shore were carrying a torch. At two o'clock a sailor sighted land.

The morning light of Friday, October 12, 1492, showed the Spaniards a beautiful little island. Columbus dressed himself in scarlet, and planted the Spanish standard on the shore, throwing himself on the earth and kissing it, while the naked Indians wondered whether these men in bright armor had flown from the skies in their winged boats or had sailed down upon the clouds. The sailors, lately so ready to cast Columbus into the sea, now crowded about him, embracing him and kissing his hands.

When the Indians had recovered from their first surprise, they visited the ships, some of them in canoes, and others by swimming. They brought with them a ball of cotton yarn, bread made from roots, and some tame parrots, which, with a few golden ornaments, they exchanged for caps, glass beads, tiny bells, and other trifles, with which they could adorn themselves.

The island which Columbus first discovered was a small one, which he called San Salvador, but we do not now know which of the West India Islands it was. He thought that he was on the coast of Asia. But where were the rich islands and great cities and houses roofed with gold, of which Marco Polo had written two hundred years before?

From island to island Columbus sailed, looking for these things, not knowing that they were thousands of miles away. Finding the island of Cuba very large, he concluded that it was a part of the mainland of Asia.

Columbus After the Discovery of America

Columbus was very kind to the natives. At one time a poor savage was captured by the sailors and brought to Columbus, who was standing on the high after-castle of the ship. The terrified Indian sought to gain his favor by presenting the great man with a ball of cotton yarn. Columbus refused the present, but he put upon the Indian's head a pretty colored cap; he hung bells in his ears, and tied strings of green beads about his arms. Then he sent the simple creature ashore, where his friends were afterward seen admiring his ornaments.

At another time the sailors picked up an Indian who was crossing in an open canoe a wide tract of water from one island to another. This man had a piece of cassava bread and a gourd of water for his sea stores. He also had a bit of red paint with which to decorate his face before appearing among strangers, and a string of beads procured from the white men. He was rowing to a neighboring island to carry the news of the coming of the Spaniards. His canoe was taken on board, he was fed with the best food of the ship, and put ashore at his destination.

Having got one of his vessels ashore on the coast of Haiti, which he called Hispaniola, Columbus built a fort of the timber from the wrecked vessel and left here a little colony.

But now he began to think of carrying home the good news of his great discovery. In January, 1493, he set sail for Spain. On the 12th of January, when all were looking forward to a joyful return, a terrific storm threatened to wreck the ship and to bury in the ocean all memory of the great discovery. Prayers were said and vows were made, for the safety of the ship.

To preserve the memory of his discovery if all else should be lost, Columbus wrote two accounts of it, which he inclosed in cakes of wax and put into two barrels. One of these was thrown into the sea; the other was set upon the stern of the vessel, that it might float off if the ship should go down. He hoped that one of these barrels might drift to the coast of Europe and be found.

Columbus at length reached the islands called the Azores. Here, when the storm had abated, some of his men went ashore to perform their vows at a little chapel, and were made prisoners by the Portuguese governor. Having got out of this difficulty, Columbus put to sea and met another gale, which split his sails and threatened to wreck the vessel. He finally came to anchor in a Portuguese port, where he no doubt felt some exultation in showing what Portugal had lost by refusing his offers.

In April he reached Barcelona, a Spanish city, and made his entry in a triumphal procession. At the head marched the Indians whom he had brought back with him. These were well smeared with paint and decorated with the feathers of tropical birds and with golden ornaments. Then parrots and stuffed birds were borne in the procession with articles of gold. Columbus followed, escorted by Spanish knights proud to do him honor. Ferdinand and Isabella received him under a canopy of gold brocade. As a mark of special honor, they caused him to sit down while he related his discoveries.

This was the happiest moment in the troubled life of Columbus. He who had been thought insane was now the most honored man in Spain.

The rest of his story is mostly a story of misfortunes. The people in his first colony on the island of Hispaniola quarreled among themselves and maltreated the Indians, until the latter fell on them and killed them all. The second colony was also unfortunate. Columbus was not a wise governor, and he had many troubles in trying to settle a new country with unruly and avaricious people.

An officer sent out to inquire into the disorders in the colony sent Columbus home in chains. The people were shocked at this treatment of the great navigator, and so were the king and queen, who ordered the chains removed. When Columbus appeared before Isabella and saw tears in her eyes, he threw himself on his knees, while his utterance was choked by his sobs.

After this he was not permitted to return to his colony; but in 1502 he made his fourth voyage to America, trying to find a way to get through the mainland of South American in order to reach India, which he thought must lie just beyond. He was at length forced to run his worm-eaten vessel aground near the shore of the island of Jamaica. Thatched cabins were built on the deck of the stranded ship, and here Columbus, a bed-ridden invalid, lived miserably for a year.

One faithful follower, named Diaz, traded a brass basin, a coat, and his two shirts, to an Indian chief for a canoe, in which after horrible suffering Diaz reach Hispaniola. Meantime the men on the wrecked ship got provisions from the Indians in exchange for trinkets. Some of the men ran away from Columbus and lived with the savages.

The Indians now got tired of providing food in exchange for toys, and Columbus and his men were at the point of starvation. Knowing that an eclipse of the moon was about to take place, he told the Indians that a certain god would punish them if they did not provide for him, and, as a sign, he said the moon would lose its light and change color that very night. No sooner did the eclipse appear, than the Indians brought him all the provisions at hand, and the Spaniards did not lack after that.

Help at length reached Columbus, and he returned to Spain broken in health and spirits. Queen Isabella, who had been his best friend, died soon after his return. Columbus died on the 20th of May, 1506. He believed to the last that he had discovered the eastern parts of Asia. He never knew that he had found a new continent.

John Cabot and his Son Sebastian

The food eaten four or five hundred years ago was mostly coarse and unwholesome. The people were therefore very fond of all sorts of spices which they mixed with almost everything they ate. These spices were brought from Asia by caravans. It was chiefly to get to the land of spices by sea that Prince Henry the Navigator tried to send ships around the southern point of Africa. Columbus had also tried to reach the "Spice Islands" of Asia in his voyage to the west.

Now another Italian was to try it. This man was John Cabot. Like Columbus, he was probably born in or near the city of Genoa; like Columbus, he thought much about geography as it was then understood; and, like Columbus, he was a great traveler. He moved to Venice and then to Bristol in England.

The Italian merchants traveled farther than any others in that day. One of Cabot's long trading journeys had carried him into Arabia as far as the city of Mecca. Here he saw the caravans that brought their loads of costly spices on the backs of camels from the countries of the East. Now the people of Europe in Cabot's time, having very few printed books, knew almost nothing about these far-away Eastern countries.

"Where do these spices come from?" Cabot asked of the men belonging to the caravan.

They answered that they brought them from a country far to the east of Mecca, where they bought spices of other caravans which brought them from a land yet farther to the east. From this Cabot reasoned as Columbus had done, that, if he should sail to the west far enough, he would get round the world to the land of spices. It would be something like going about a house to come in by the back door.

While Cabot was living in England there came great news out of Spain. One Christopher Columbus, it was said, had discovered the coasts of India by sailing to the westward, for Columbus thought the land he had found a part of India. When this was told in England, people thought it "a thing more divine than human to sail by the west into the east." And when Cabot heard the story, there arose in his heart, as he said, "a great flame of desire to do some notable thing."

While Columbus had waited in discouragement for Ferdinand and Isabella to accept his project, he had sent his brother Bartholomew Columbus to

Henry the Seventh, then King of England, to offer the plan to him. What answer the king gave to Bartholomew is not known, for, before the latter got back to Spain, Christopher Columbus had returned from his first voyage.

But now for this same King Henry of England Cabot offered to make a voyage like that of Columbus. As the Atlantic had already once been crossed, the king readily agreed to allow Cabot to sail under his authority.

In May, 1497, Cabot set sail from Bristol in a small vessel with eighteen men, mostly Englishmen. Cabot sailed much farther north than Columbus, and he appears to have discovered first the island of Cape Breton, now part of the Dominion of Canada. He went ashore on the 24th of June, and planted a large cross and the flag of England, as well as the flag of St. Mark, the patron saint of Venice. He also discovered the mainland of North America. Cabot was thus the first to see the American continent. Columbus discovered the mainland of South America a year later. Cabot did not see any Indians, but he brought back some of their traps for catching wild animals.

He got back to England in August, having been gone but three months. He brought news that he had discovered the territory of the Emperor of China. The king gave him a pension, he dressed himself in silks, and was called "The Great Admiral." It is to be feared this sudden rise in the world puffed him up a great deal. To one of his companions he promised an island, and another island he was going to bestow on his barber! On the strength of these promises, both of these men set themselves up for counts!

That there were many fish on the new coast was a fact which impressed the practical Bristol people, though Cabot had no thought of engaging in fishery. He imagined that by sailing a little farther south than before he might come to the large island that Marco Polo called Cipango, and we now call Japan. He did not know that the far-off country he had seen was not half so far away as Japan. Cabot believed that all the spices and precious stones in the world came from Cipango.

King Henry the Seventh fitted out Cabot with another and much larger expedition. This expedition went far to the north along the coast of America, and then away to the south as far as the shores of what is now the State of North Carolina. Cabot found Indians dressed in skins, and possessing no metal but a little copper. He found no gold, and he brought back no spices. The island of Cipango and the territories of the Emperor of China he looked for in vain, though he was sure that he had reached the coast of Asia.

Cabot's crew brought back stories of seas so thick with codfish that their vessels were made to move more slowly by them. They even told of bears swimming out into the sea and catching codfish in their claws. But the

English people lost interest in voyages that brought neither gold nor spices, and we do not know anything more about John Cabot.

John Cabot's second son, Sebastian, who was with him on this voyage, became, like his father, famous for his knowledge of geography, and was sometimes employed by the King of Spain and sometimes by the King of England. He promoted expeditions to try to find a way to China by the north of Europe. When a very old man he took a great interest in the sailing of a new expedition of discovery, and visited with a company of ladies and gentlemen the Search-thrift, a little vessel starting on a voyage of exploration to the northeast. Having tasted of "such good cheer" as the sailors could make aboard the ship, and after making them liberal presents, the little company went ashore and dined at the sign of the "Christopher," where the lively old gentleman for joy, as it is said, at the "towardness" of the discovery, danced with the rest of "the young company," after which he and his friends departed, "most gently commending" the sailors to the care of God.

Captain John Smith

On the estate of Lord Willoughby, in the eastern part of England, there was a family of poor tenants named Smith, who had a son born in 1579. The named him John. John Smith is the most common of names, but this was the most uncommon of all the John Smiths. He was apprenticed to learn a trade, but he ran away from his master and became, for a while, a servant to Lord Willoughby, who was going to Holland.

Like most runaway boys, he found the world a hard place, and had to lead a very rough-and-tumble life. He enlisted as a soldier; he was shipwrecked; he was robbed and reduced to beggary; and, if we may believe his own story, he was once pitched into the sea by a company of pilgrims, who thought that he had caused the storm, like Jonah in the Bible. This must have happened not far from shore, for he reached land without the aid of a whale, and went into the war against the Turks. There he killed three Turks in single combat, and cut off their heads, but Captain John Smith came near losing his own head in the fight with the last one.

The Turks captured Smith afterwards and made him a slave. His Turkish master was very cruel, and put an iron collar on his neck. While Smith was thrashing wheat one day with his dog collar on, the Turk began to thrash him. Smith grew angry, and, leaving the wheat, hit his master with the flail, killing him on the spot. Then he took a bag of wheat for food, mounted his master's horse and escaped to the wilderness, and got out of Turkey.

When, at last, Captain Smith got back to England with his wonderful budget of stories about narrow escapes and bloody fights, he probably found it hard to settle down to a peaceful life. The English people were just then talking a great deal about settling a colony in North America, which was quite wild and almost wholly unexplored. Nothing suited the wandering and daring Captain Smith better. He joined the company which set sail for America, in three little ships, in 1606. The largest of these was called the Susan Constant.

I am sorry to say the people sent out in this first company were what we should call nowadays a hard set. They were most of them men who knew nothing about work. They had heard how the Spaniards grew rich from the gold and silver in South America, and they expected to pick up gold without trouble.

The colony was settled at a place called Jamestown. Soon after the settlers landed the Indians attacked them while they were unarmed, and the settlers might all have been put to death with the bows and arrows and war clubs of the savages, if the people on one of the ships had not fired a cross-bar shot—such as you see in the picture. This cross-bar shot happened to cut down a limb of a tree over the heads of the Indians. When they heard the noise of the cannon, like thunder, and saw the tree tops come tumbling on their heads, the savages thought it was time to make good use of their heels.

The people of that day did not know how to plant colonies, and the lack of good food and shelter caused the death of more than half of the Jamestown settlers. The Indians who lived near them had fields of Indian corn, whose streaming blades and waving tassels were a strange sight to Englishmen. When at last the corn was ripe, Captain John Smith set sail in a small boat and traded a lot of trinkets to the Indians for corn, and so saved the lives of many of the people.

The English thought America was only a narrow strip of land. They were still looking for a way to India, as Columbus had looked for one more than a hundred years before. The King of England had told them to explore any river coming from the northwest. Smith therefore set out to sail up the little Chickahom'iny River to find the Pacific Ocean, not knowing that this ocean was nearly three thousand miles away.

The daring captain left his two men in charge of the boat while he went on farther. The Indians killed the men and then pursued Smith. Smith had taken an Indian prisoner, and he saved himself by putting this prisoner between him and his enemies. But the Indians caught Smith after he had fled into a swamp, where he sank up to his waist in the mud, so that he could neither fight nor run. He made friends with the head Indian of the party by giving him a pocket compass and trying to explain its use.

As all the Indians had a great curiosity to see a white man, Smith was marched from one Indian village to another; but he was treated with a great deal of respect. Perhaps the Indians thought that men who sailed in big canoes and discharged guns that blazed and smoked and made a noise like thunder and knocked the trees down, must have some mysterious power. But they also thought that if they could persuade the white people to give them some big guns they could easily conquer all the Indian tribes with which they were at war.

The Indians surrounded Smith with curious charms by way of finding out whether he was friendly to them or not. They fed him very well; but Smith, who was as ignorant of Indians as they were of white people, thought that they were fattening him to eat him, so he did not have much appetite.

Powhatan was the name of the great chief of these Indians. This chief set Smith free. He sent some men along with him on his return to Jamestown to bring back two cannons and a grindstone in exchange for the prisoner; but the Indians found these things rather too heavy to carry, and they were forced to return with nothing but trinkets.

Captain Smith seems to have been the best man to control the unruly settlers and manage the Indians. The people in England who had sent out this colony thought they could make the chief, Powhatan, friendly by sending him presents. They sent him a crown, a wash basin, and a bedstead, also a red robe, and other things quite unnecessary to a wild Indian. But when Powhatan for the first time in his life had a bedstead and a wash basin and a red gown, he thought himself so important that he would not sell corn to the settlers, who were in danger of starving. Captain Smith, however, showed him some blue glass beads, pretending that he could not sell them because they were made of some substance like the sky, and were to be worn only by the greatest princes. Powhatan became half crazy to get these precious jewels, and Smith brought a large boat-load of corn for a pound or two of beads.

More about Captain John Smith

The two best things about Captain John Smith were, that he was never idle and he never gave up. He was a good man to have in a colony, for he was always trying to find out something new or to accomplish some great thing. He had not found a way to China in the swamps on the Chickahominy River; he had only found a mudhole, and got himself captured by the Indians. But he thought he might find the Pacific Ocean by sailing up the Chesapeake Bay. So he went twice up this bay, exploring at last to the very head of it. Of course, he did not find a way into the Pacific Ocean. We know well enough nowadays that China is not anywhere in the neighborhood of Baltimore. But Smith made a good map of the great bay, and he bought corn from the Indians, and so kept the colony alive. This was better than finding a way to China, if he had only known it.

In living in an open boat and sailing among Indians that were very suspicious and unfriendly, Smith and his men had to suffer many hardships. They were sometimes nearly wrecked by storms, and once when their sail had been torn to pieces they patched it with the shirts off their backs. Their bread was spoiled by the splashing of the salt water, and they suffered to much from thirst that at one time they would have been willing to give a barrel of gold, if they had only had it, for a drink of puddle water. Sometimes, when sleeping on the ground, they got so cold that they were forced to get up in the night and move their fire, so that they could like down on the warm earth where the fire had been.

At one place the Indians shot arrows at them from the trees. Then they tried to get the Englishmen to come on

shore by dancing with baskets in their hands. Captain Smith says that he felt sure they had nothing in their baskets but villainy. So he had his men fire off their guns. The noise of the guns so frightened the savages that they all dropped to the ground and then fled into the woods. Smith and his men now ventured ashore and left presents of beads, little bells, and looking-glasses in their wigwams. Pleased with these things, the Indians became friendly and fell to trading.

Once, when many of Captain Smith's men were ill, the Indians attacked him. Smith put his sick men under a tarpaulin, and mounted their hats on sticks among his well men, so that the boat appeared to have its full force. Having procured Indian shields of wickerwork, Captain Smith put them along the side of his boat, so as to fight from behind them. But he generally made friends with the Indian tribes, and he came back to Jamestown with plenty of corn and furs.

Powhatan, the greatest of the Indian chiefs, wanted to get the arms of the white men. Muskets, swords, and pistols were now and then stolen by the Indians, and Captain Smith tried to put a stop to this thievery. Two Indians who were brothers stole a pistol. They were captured, and one of them was put into prison, while the other was sent to get the pistol. The one in the prison was allowed a fire of charcoal, to keep him from freezing. When his brother came back the prison was found smothered by the gas from the charcoal fire. The other poor fellow was heartbroken; but Captain Smith succeeded in reviving the one that had been smothered. From this the Indians concluded that he was not only a great brave, but a great medicine man as well, who could bring dead people to life.

At another time an Indian stole a bag of gunpowder, which was a thing of wonder to the savages. He also stole a piece of armor at the same time. He had seen white men dry their powder when wet by putting it into a piece of armor and holding it over the fire. He tried to do the same thing; but the fire was too hot for the powder, and the Indian was treated to a very great surprise. This terrified the savages for a time.

In 1609 there were many newcomers, and Captain Smith's enemies got control of the colony. They sent Smith home, and he never saw Virginia again.

Captain Smith afterwards sailed on a voyage to New England in 1614. While his men caught and salted fish to pay for the expense of the voyage, Smith sailed in an open boat along the New England coast. He traded with the Indians, giving them beads and other trinkets for furs. He also made the first good map of the coast. After he had returned to England with furs, Hunt, who was captain of his second ship, coaxed twenty-four Indians on board and then sailed away with them to Spain. Here he made sale of his shipload of salted fish, and began to sell the poor Indians for slaves. Some good monks, finding out what he was doing, stopped him and took the Indians into their convent to make Christians of them. One of these Indians, named Squanto, afterwards found his way to England, and from there was taken back to America.

Captain Smith tried very hard to persuade English people to plant a colony in New England. He finally set out with only sixteen men to begin a settlement there. He had made friends with the New England Indians, and he was sure that with a few men he could still succeed in planting a colony.

But he had very bad luck. He first lost the masts of his vessels in a storm. He returned to England again and set sail in a smaller ship. He was then chased by a pirate vessel. Smith found, on hailing this ship, that some of the men on board had been soldiers under him in the Turkish wars. They proposed to him to be their captain, but he did not want to command such rogues.

Smith's little vessel had no sooner got away from these villains, than he was chased by a French ship. He had to threaten to blow up his ship to get his men to fight. He escaped again, but the next time he was met by a fleet of French privateers. They made Smith come aboard one of their vessels to show his papers. After they had got him out of his ship they held him prisoner and took possession of his cargo. They afterwards agreed to let him have his vessel again, as he was still determined to sail to New England; but his men wanted to turn back; so, while Smith was on the French ship, his own men ray away with his vessel and got back to England. Thus his plan for a colony failed.

Smith spent his summer in the French fleet. When the French privateers were fighting with an English vessel they made Smith a prisoner in the cabin; but when they fought with Spanish ships they would put Smith at the guns and make him fight with them. Smith reached England at last, and had the satisfaction of having some of his runaway sailors put into prison. He never tried to plant another colony, though he was very much pleased with the success of the Plymouth colony which settled in New England a few years later than this. This brave, roving, fighting, boasting captain died in 1631, when he was fifty-two years old.

The Story of Pocahontas

While Captain John Smith was a prisoner among the Indians of Powhatan's tribe, he made the acquaintance of that chief's daughter, Pocahontas, a little girl of ten or twelve years of age, with whom he was very much pleased. Years afterwards, he said that Powhatan had at one time determined to put him to death; but when Captain Smith's head was laid upon some stones, and Indians stood ready to beat out his brains, Pocahontas laid her head on his, so that they could not kill Captain Smith without striking her; seeing which, Powhatan let him live. Captain Smith said nothing about this occurrence in the first accounts of his captivity, and many people think that it never happened.

But it is certain that, whether Pocahontas saved his life at this time or not, he was much attached to her, and she became very fond of going to Jamestown, where she played with the boys in the street. When the settlers were in danger of starving, she brought them food. When a messenger was sent from Jamestown to carry an important message to Captain Smith, then in Powhatan's country, she hid the man, and got him through in spite of Powhatan's desire to kill him. When the Indians intended to kill Captain Smith, she went to his tent at night and gave him warning. Captain Smith offered her trinkets as a reward, but she refused them, with tears in her eyes, saying that Powhatan would kill her if he knew of her coming there. These are the stories told of her in Captain Smith's history. And when a number of white men then in the Indian country were put to death, she saved the life of a white boy named Henry Spelman by sending him away.

When Captain Smith had been in the colony two years, ships came from London with many hundreds of people. The ships that brought this company to Jamestown in 1609 were under the command of men that were enemies of Captain Smith, who had come to be governor of the colony. These men resolved to depose John Smith, so as to get the government of Jamestown into their own hands. Smith, having been injured by an explosion of gunpowder, consented to go back to England. His enemies sent charges against him. One of these charges was that he wished to marry Pocahontas, who was now growing up, and thus to get possession of the colony by claiming it for the daughter of Powhatan, whom the English regarded as a kind of king.

The colony had every reason to be sorry that Captain Smith was sent away. The men left in charge managed badly, Powhatan ceased to be friendly, and his little daughter did not come to see the English people any more. The people of Jamestown were now so afraid of the Indians that they dared not venture outside the town. Soon all of their food was gone, and they had eaten up their horses. Some of the people were killed by the Indians; some fled in one of the ships and became pirates; and great numbers of them died of hunger.

Ships arrived at last, bringing help to the colony. Under one governor and another Jamestown suffered many troubles from sickness and from the Indians. There was in the colony a sea captain named Argall, who thought that, if he could get Pocahontas into his power, her father, the great chief Powhatan, might be persuaded to be peaceable.

Pocahontas was by this time a young woman of about eighteen. She was visiting an old chief named Japazaws, who lived on the Potomac River. Argall was trading with the Indians at Japazaws's town. He told Japazaws that, if he would bring Pocahontas on board his ship, he would give him a copper kettle. Every Indian wanted to have a copper kettle, of all things. Japazaws and his wife, pretending that they wished to see the vessel, coaxed Pocahontas to go with them. Argall refused to let her go ashore again, and carried her to Jamestown a prisoner.

Here she stayed a year. The English people in Jamestown refused to give her up unless Powhatan would return some guns which the Indians had taken. There was an Englishman living at Jamestown, named John Rolfe, who fell in love with Pocahontas, and proposed to marry her. When word was sent to Powhatan of this, he readily agreed to the marriage, and an old uncle and two brothers of Pocahontas went down to Jamestown to attend the wedding. Pocahontas, having been instructed in the Christian religion, was baptized in the little church, and married to Rolfe in 1614. Her real name was Matoax, but her father called her Pocahontas. When she was baptized, she took the name of Rebecca.

The marriage of Pocahontas brought peace with the Indians. In 1616, with her little baby boy, Pocahontas was taken to England. Here she was called "the Lady Rebecca," and treated with great respect as the daughter of a king.

The people at Jamestown had told Pocahontas that John Smith was dead. When she saw him alive in England, she was very much offended. She fell into such a pout that for some time she would not speak to anybody. Then she announced her intention of calling Captain Smith her father, after the Indian plan of adoption.

She was greatly petted by the king and queen and all the great people. The change from a smoky bark hut to high life in England must have been very great, but she surprised everybody by the quickness with which she learned to behave rightly in any company. She was much pleased with England, and was sorry to go back. When she was ready to sail, she was attacked by smallpox, and died.

Her little boy was now left in England. Captain Argall, who had made Pocahontas prisoner, was now made Governor of Virginia. He was a very dishonest man, and he and some partners of his appear to have had a scheme to get possession of the colony by claiming it for the child of Pocahontas as the grandson of "King Powhatan." Argall sent word to England that the Indians had resolved to sell no more land, but to keep it all for this child. This was, no doubt, a falsehood. Argall was a bad governor, and he was soon recalled, and a better man took his place. The son of Pocahontas returned to Virginia when he was grown.

But when Pocahontas was dead, and Powhatan also, there was nothing to keep the Indians quiet, and in 1622 they suddenly fell upon the settlement and killed more than three hundred people in one day. Long and bloody wars followed, but the colony of Virginia lived through them all.

Henry Hudson

Three hundred years ago England was rather poor in people and in money. Spain had become rich and important by her gold mines in the West Indies and the central parts of America. Portugal had been enriched by finding a way around Africa to India, where many things such as silks and spices were bought to be sold in Europe at high prices. Some thoughtful men in England had an idea that as the Portuguese had reached India by sailing round the Eastern Continent on the south, the English might find a way to sail to India around the northern part of Europe and Asia. By this means the English ships would also be able to get the precious things to be found in the East.

For this purpose some London merchants founded the Mus'-co-vy Company, with old Sebastian Cabot at its head. This Muscovy Company had not succeeded in finding a way to China round the north of Europe, but in trying to do this its ships had opened a valuable trade with Russia, or Muscovy as it was then called, which was a country but little known before.

One of the founders of this Muscovy Company was a rich man named Henry Hudson. It is thought that he was the grandfather of Henry Hudson, the explorer. The merchants who made up this company were in the habit of sending out their sons, while they were boys, in the ships of the company, to learn to sail vessels and to gain a knowledge of the languages and habits of trade in distant countries. Henry was sent to sea while a lad, and was no doubt taught by the ship captains all about sailing vessels. When he grew to be a man, he wished to make himself famous by finding a northern way to China.

In the spring of 1607, almost four months after Captain Smith had left London with the colony bound for Jamestown, his friend Hudson was sent out by the Muscovy Company to try once more for a passage to China. He had only a little ship, which was named Hopewell, and he had but ten men, including his own son John Hudson. He found that there was no way to India by the north pole. But he went farther north than any other man had gone.

Hudson made an important discovery on this voyage. He found whales in the Arctic Seas, and the Muscovy Company now fitted out whaling ships to catch them. The next year the brave Hudson tried to pass between Spitz-berg'-en and Nova Zembla, but he was again turned back by the walls of ice that fence in the frozen pole.

By this time the Muscovy Company was discouraged, and gave up trying to get to India by going round the north of Europe. They thought it better to make money out of the whale fishery that Hudson had found. But in Holland there was the Dutch East India Company, which sent ships round Africa to India. They had heard of the voyages of Hudson, who had got the name of "the bold Englishman." The Dutch Company was afraid that the English, with Hudson's help, might find a nearer way by the north, and so get the trade away from them. So they sent for "the bold Englishman," and hired him to find this new route for them.

Hudson left Amsterdam in 1609 in a yacht called "The Half Moon." He sailed round Norway and found his old enemy the ice as bad as ever about Nova Zembla. Just before leaving home Hudson had received a letter from his friend Captain John Smith, in Virginia, telling him that there was a strait leading into the Pacific Ocean, to the north of Virginia. Hudson persuaded his men to turn about and sail with him to America to look for the way to India that Smith had written about.

So they turned to the westward and sailed to Newfoundland, and thence down the coast until they were opposite James River. Then Hudson turned north again, and began to look for a gateway through this wild and unknown coast. He sailed into Delaware Bay, as ships do now on their way to Philadelphia. Then he sailed out again and followed the shore till he came to the opening by which thousands of ships nowadays go into New York.

He passed into New York Bay, where no vessel had ever been before. He said it was "a very good land to fall in with, and a pleasant land to see." The New Jersey Indians swarmed about the ship dressed in fur robes and feather mantles, and wearing copper necklaces. Hudson thought some of the waterways about New York harbor must lead into the Pacific.

He sent men out in a boat to examine the bays and rivers. They declared that the land was "as pleasant with grass and flowers as ever they had seen, and very sweet smells." But before they got back, some Indians attacked the boat and killed one man by shooting him with an arrow.

When the Indians came round the ship again, Hudson made two of them prisoners, and dressed them up in red coats. The rest he drove away. As he sailed farther up from the sea, twenty-eight dugout canoes filled with men, women, and children, paddled about the ship. The white men traded with them, giving them trinkets for oysters and beans, but none were allowed to come aboard. As the ship sailed on up the river that we now call the Hudson, the two Indian prisoners saw themselves carried farther and farther from their home. One morning they jumped out of a porthole and swam ashore, without even stopping to say good-by. They stood on the bank and mocked the men on the Half Moon as she sailed away up the river.

Hudson's ship anchored again opposite the Catskill Mountains, and here he found some very friendly Indians, who brought corn, pumpkins, and tobacco to sell to the crew. Still farther up the river Hudson visited a tribe on shore, and wondered at their great heaps of corn and beans. The chief lived in a round bark house. Captain Hudson was made to sit on a mat and eat from a red wooden bowl. The Indians wished him to stay all night; they broke their arrows and threw them into the fire, to show their friendliness.

Hudson found the river growing shallower. When he got near where Albany now stands he sent a rowboat yet higher up. Then he concluded that this was not the way to the Pacific. He turned round and sailed down the river, and then across the ocean to England. The Half Moon returned to Holland, and the Dutch sent out other ships to trade in the river which Hudson had found. In the course of time they planted a colony where New York now stands.

Captain Hudson did not try to go round the north of Europe any more. But the next spring he sailed in an English ship to look for a way round the north side of the American Continent. On this voyage he discovered the great bay that is now called Hudson Bay.

In this bay he spent the winter. His men suffered from hunger and sickness. In the summer of 1611, after he had, with tears in his eyes, divided his last bread with his men, these wicked fellows put him into a boat with some sick sailors and cast them all adrift in the great bay.

The men on the ship shot some birds for food, but in a fight with the Indians some of the leaders in the plot against Hudson were killed. The seamen, as they sailed homeward, grew so weak from hunger that they had to sit down to steer the vessel. When at last Juet, the mate, who had put Hudson overboard, had himself died of hunger, and all the rest had lain down in despair to die, they were saved by meeting another ship.

Captain Myles Standish

Thirteen years after the first settlement at Jamestown a colony was planted in New England. We have seen that the rough-and-ready John Smith was the man who had to deal with the Indians in Virginia. So the first colony in New England had also its soldier, a brave and rather hot-tempered little man—Captain Standish.

Myles Standish was born in England in 1584. He became a soldier, and, like John Smith, went to fight in the Low Country—that is in what we now call Holland—which was at that time fighting to gain its liberty from Spain.

The Government of Holland let people be religious in their own way, as our country does now. In nearly all other countries at that time people were punished if they did not worship after the manner of the established church of the land. A little band of people in the north of England had set up a church of their own. For this they were persecuted. In order to get away from their troubles they sold their houses and goods and went over to Holland. These are the people that we now call "the Pilgrims," because of their wanderings.

Captain Standish, who was also from the north of England, met these countrymen of his in Holland. He liked their simple service and honest ways, and he lived among them though he did not belong to their church.

The Pilgrims remained about thirteen years in Holland. By this time they had made up their minds to seek a new home in the wild woods of America. About a hundred of them bade the rest good-by and sailed for America in the Mayflower in 1620. As there might be some fighting to do, the brave soldier Captain Myles Standish went along with them.

The ship first reached land at Cape Cod. Captain Standish and sixteen men landed, and marched along the shore looking for a place to settle. In one spot they found the ground freshly patted down. Digging here, they discovered Indian baskets filled with corn. Indian corn is an American plant, and they had never before seen it. The beautiful grains, red, yellow, and white, were a "goodly sight," as they said. Some of this corn they took with them to plant the next spring. The Pilgrims paid the Indians for this seed corn when they found the right owners.

Standish made his next trip in a boat. This time he found some Indian wigwams covered and lined with mats. In December, Captain Standish made a third trip along the shore. It was now so cold that the spray froze to the clothes of his men while they rowed. At night they slept behind a little barricade made of logs and boughs, so as to be ready if the Indians should attack them.

One morning some of the men carried all their guns down to the water-side and laid them in the boat, in order to be ready for a start as soon as breakfast should be finished. But all at once there broke on their ears a sound they had never heard before. It was the wild war whoop of a band of Indians whose arrows rained around Standish and his men. Some of the men ran to the boat for their guns, at which the Indians raised a new yell and sent another lot of arrows flying after them. But once the white men were in possession of their guns, they fired a volley which made the Indians take to their heels. One uncommonly brave Indian lingered behind a tree to fight it out alone; but when a bullet struck the tree and sent bits of bark and splinters rattling about his head, he thought better of it, and ran after his friends into the woods.

Captain Standish and his men at length came to a place which John Smith, when he explored the coast, had called Plymouth. Here the Pilgrims found a safe harbor for ships and some running brooks from which they might get fresh water. They therefore selected it for their landing place. There had once been an Indian town here, but all the Indians in it had died of a pestilence three or four years before this time. The Indian cornfields were now lying idle, which was lucky for the Pilgrims, since otherwise they would have had to chop down trees to clear a field.

The Pilgrims landed on the 21st day of December, in our way of counting, or, as some say, the 22nd. They built some rough houses, using paper dipped in oil instead of window glass. But the bad food and lack of warm houses or clothing brought on a terrible sickness, so that here, as at Jamestown, one half of the people died in the first year. Captain Standish lost his wife, but he himself was well enough to be a kind nurse to the sick. Though he was born of a high family, he did not neglect to do the hardest and most disagreeable work for his sick and dying neighbors.

As there were not many houses, the people in Plymouth were divided into nineteen families, and the single men had to live with one or another of these families. A young man named John Alden was assigned to live in Captain Standish's house. Some time after Standish's wife died the captain thought he would like to marry a young woman named Priscilla Mullins. But as Standish was much older than Priscilla, and a rough-spoken soldier in his ways, he asked his young friend Alden to go to the Mullins house and try to secure Priscilla for him.

It seems that John Alden loved Priscilla, and she did not dislike him. But Standish did not know this, and poor Alden felt bound to do as the captain requested. In that day the father of the young lady was asked first. So Alden went to Mr. Mullins and told him what a brave man Captain Standish was. Then he asked if Captain Standish might marry Priscilla.

"I have no objection to Captain Standish," said Priscilla's father, "but this is a matter she must decide."

So he called in his daughter, and told her in Alden's presence that the young man had come to ask her hand in marriage with the brave Captain Standish. Priscilla had no notion of marrying the captain. She looked at the young man a moment, and then said:

"Why don't you speak for yourself, John?"

The result was that she married John Alden, and Captain Standish married another woman. You may read this story, a little changed, in Longfellow's poem called "The Courtship of Miles Standish."

Myles Standish and the Indians

The Indians, having got one taste of the firearms of the white men, were afraid to attack Plymouth. But they thought that they might get rid of the white men by witchcraft. So they held what they called a "powwow" in a big swamp, to persuade the spirits to kill or drive away the newcomers. Sometimes the Pilgrims would see some Indians on a hill-top near Plymouth. But the savages always ran away as soon as they were discovered. Perhaps they came to see whether the Plymouth people had all been killed by the spirits.

But in the spring a chief from a place farther east came to visit the Indians near Plymouth. He had met English fishermen and learned a little English. He was not afraid to visit the white men. Walking boldly into the little town, he said, "Welcome, Englishmen." The Pilgrims were surprised to hear two English words from the mouth of an Indian.

They treated this Indian well, and he came again bringing an Indian named Squanto who could speak more English. Squanto, who had lived at Plymouth, was one of the Indians carried away to Spain by Captain Hunt. From Spain he had been taken to England, and then brought back to America. When he got home to Plymouth he found that all the people of his village had died of the pestilence.

Squanto now came again to the old home of his people at Plymouth and lived with the Pilgrims. He showed the English a way to catch eels by treading them out of the mud with his feet. He knew the woods and waters well, and he showed them how to hunt and fish. He taught them how to plant Indian corn as the Indians did, putting a fish or two in every hill for manure, and then watching the fields for a while to keep the wolves from digging up the buried fish. Without the seed corn and the help of Squanto the whole colony would have starved.

Squanto liked to make himself important among the Indians by boasting of the power of his friends the white men. He talked about the dreadful gunpowder kept in the cellar at Plymouth. He also told them that the horrid pestilence was kept in the same cellar with the powder.

Massasoit, the chief of Squanto's tribe, came to see the Pilgrims, bringing some other Indians with him. They were taken into the largest house in Plymouth and seated on a green mat and some cushions. The Governor of the colony was then brought in while the trumpets were blowing and the drums beating. This parade pleased the Indians, but they were much afraid of the Plymouth people. Afterwards the Pilgrims sent Massasoit a red cotton coat and a copper chain, and by degrees a firm friendship was made between him and the white men.

Captain Standish was a little man, and one of his enemies once nicknamed him "Captain Shrimp." But the Indians soon learned to be afraid of him. When a chief near by threatened to trouble the Pilgrims and kill Squanto, Standish marched to the spot and surrounded his wigwam. Having fired on the Indians and frightened them, he took three whom he had wounded back to Plymouth with him. The white people cured their wounds and sent them home again.

The Nar-ra-gan'-sett Indians were enemies of Massasoit. None of their people had died of the pestilence, and they were therefore stronger than Massasoit's tribe. The Narragansetts sent a bundle of arrows to Plymouth tied up in a snake's skin. Squanto told the English that this meant to say that they would come and make war on Plymouth. The Pilgrims filled the snake's skin with bullets, and sent it back. This was to say, "Shoot your arrows at us and we will kill you with our bullets." The Narragansetts were so afraid of the bullets that they sent them back to Plymouth, and there was no war.

When the Pilgrims had been settled at Plymouth more than a year, a ship brought them news of the dreadful massacre that had taken place in Virginia. The Pilgrims were afraid something of the kind might happen to them. So Captain Standish trained the Plymouth men, and they kept guard every night. They put cannon on the roof of their meetinghouse and carried their guns to church.

A company of people from England made a settlement at Weymouth, not very far from Plymouth. They were rude and familiar, and the Indians soon despised them. Some Indian warriors made a plan to kill them all. They intended to kill the Plymouth people at the same time. But Massasoit told the Pilgrims about it, and said they must go and kill the leaders before they had a chance to kill the white men.

Captain Standish set out for the colony at Weymouth. He took but few men, so that the Indians might not guess what he came for. But they saw that the little captain was very "angry in his heart," as they said. Seeing how few his men were, they tried to frighten him.

One of these Indians named Wittamut sharpened the knife which he wore hanging about his neck. While sharpening it he said to Captain Standish: "This is a good knife. On the handle is the picture of a woman's face. But I have another knife at home with which I have killed both Frenchmen and

Englishmen. That knife has a man's face on it. After a while these two will get married."

A large Indian named Pecksuot said: "You are a captain, but you are a little man. I am not a chief, but I am strong and brave."

It was now a question whether Standish would attack the Indians or wait for them to begin. One day when Wittamut, Pecksuot, and two other Indians were in the room with Standish and some of his men, the captain made a signal, and himself snatched the knife that hung on Pecksuot's neck and stabbed him to death after a terrible struggle. His men killed the other Indians in the same way. The rest of their tribe fled to the woods for fear, and after that the English were called "stabbers" in the Indian language.

The Pilgrims were often very near to starvation during the first years after they settled at Plymouth. At one time they lived on clams and lobsters and such fish as they could catch. Standish made many voyages along the coast, trading with the Indians for furs, which were sent to England and exchanged for whatever the settlers might need.

A few years after the Pilgrims settled Plymouth people began to settle near them, and in 1630 there came over a large number of people, who founded Boston and other Massachusetts towns. Captain Standish lived to be more than seventy years old and to see many thousands of people in New England. He owned a place at Duxbury, just across the bay from Plymouth. He died there in 1656. The hill which he owned is still called "Captain's Hill."

William Penn

William Penn, who founded Pennsylvania, was born in London, England, in 1644. He was the only son of Admiral William Penn. Admiral Penn had become a captain before he was twenty, and had distinguished himself in naval battles. He was a rich man, lived fashionably, and was received at court. He wanted to make his son William a man of importance in the world like himself. So William Penn was carefully educated. When he was at Oxford he heard a man named Thomas Loe preach against such things as the wearing of gowns by students. It had been the custom for the students in the colleges at Oxford to wear gowns; but the Puritans, who ruled England after Charles I was beheaded, forbade this, having a notion that it was wicked. When King Charles II was restored to the throne, the students were again required to put on gowns. Under the influence of Loe's preaching, Penn and some other young men refused to dress in this way, and they even went so far as to tear off the gowns of other students. For this Penn was expelled from the university.

William Penn's father was very angry with his son when he came home expelled. He was afraid that his son would join the Friends, or Quakers, who not only refused to take part in the ceremonies of the English Church, but also refused to serve the king as soldiers, believing war to be wicked. They would not make oath in court, nor would they take off their hats to anybody. Admiral Penn did not like to see his son adopt the opinions and ways of a people so much despised and persecuted.

Hoping that William would forget these impressions, he sent him to France. Here young Penn was presented at the court of Louis XIV, and here he finished his education. He then traveled in Italy, and returned to England when he was twenty years old. His father was well pleased to see that he had improved in manners, and seemed to have forgotten his Quaker ideas.

He was presented at the court of Charles II, and became a law student. He also carried dispatches from his father's fleet to the king. In 1665 the plague broke out in London, and in these sad times William Penn's religious feelings began to return.

His father, hoping to give him something else to think about, sent him to Ireland to attend to some land which belonged to the admiral. Here he was presented at the court of the viceroy, the Duke or Ormond. He served as a soldier for a little while during an insurrection. You will see that his portrait was painted in armor, after the fashion of fine gentlemen of that time. But while Penn was in Ireland, he heard that Thomas Loe, whose preaching had affected him so much when he was a student, was to preach in Cork. Penn went to hear him; all his old feelings revived, and he became a Friend. He now attended the meetings of the Friends, or Quakers, for which he was at length arrested and thrown into prison with the rest of the congregation. He was afterwards set free. His father, hearing of what his son had been doing, sent for him.

Admiral Penn was very angry with William, but he told him that he would forgive him everything else if he would take off his hat to his father, to the king, and to the king's brother, the Duke of York. William took some time to think of it, and then told his father that he could not promise even this. The admiral then turned his son out of doors. But his mother sent him money, and after a time he was allowed to come home, but not to see his father.

William Penn presently began to preach and write in favor of the doctrines of the Friends. He soon got into trouble, and was imprisoned in the Tower of London for eight months. The duke of York was a great friend of William Penn's father, and he finally got Penn released from the Tower. The father now gave up opposing his son's religion. William Penn was arrested again in about a year for preaching in the street. He was tried, and spoke for himself very boldly in court. The jury, after listening to him, would not bring in any verdict but that he was guilty of speaking in the street.

The judges were very angry with the jury, but the jurymen would not change their verdict. The judges of that day were very tyrannical. The jurymen in this case were fined, and sent to prison along with William Penn, who was imprisoned for wearing his hat in court. Soon after Penn was released, his father died. The admiral asked the Duke of York to befriend his son, who, he feared, would always be in trouble.

Penn now traveled in England, Wales, Ireland, Holland, and Germany, on his preaching journeys. He used all the influence he had at court with the king and the king's brother, the Duke of York, to get Quakers and other persecuted people out of prison.

The American colonies had come to be a place for people of all religions to flee to when they were troubled in England. Some members of the Society of Friends—Penn among others—began to be interested in West Jersey, a part of what is now the State of New Jersey, as a place of refuge for Quakers.

The English Government owed Penn's father a large sum of money. Charles II was in debt, and found it hard to pay what he owed, so at length Penn persuaded the king to grant him a tract of land on the west side of the

Delaware River. The king named this Pennsylvania, in honor of Admiral Penn. William Penn made the laws of his colony such that nobody in it would be troubled because of his religion. He sent some colonists there in 1681. Some of the people dug holes in the river bank to live in when they first reached Pennsylvania. Penn himself came the next year, and laid out a city, naming it Philadelphia, which means "Brotherly Love."

William Penn managed the Indians well, and for many years after his death Pennsylvania had no wars. Penn made a treaty with the Indians under a large elm, in 1682. The woods were filled with savages, all armed and painted. The Quakers were but a handful. They wore neither weapons nor ornaments, except that Penn had a sky-blue sash around his waist. The Indians seated themselves on the ground around their various chiefs in the form of half-moons.

When Penn was a young man he had been famous for his skill in jumping and other exercises. Finding the Indians engaged in a jumping match one day, he took part with them, and they were much pleased to have the great governor share in their sport. Pennsylvania grew much faster than any of the other colonies. The government established by Penn was free, the Indians were friendly, and the land was sold in small farms, so that poor men could own their farms. People, therefore, liked to settle in Penn's colony.

After two years William Penn went back to England. King Charles II died soon after. William Penn's friend, the Duke of York, now became king as James II, and Penn was seen a great deal in the palace. He got the Friends relieved from all their troubles, but he came to be hated a great deal by those who disliked King James. When this king was driven from England, and King William and Queen Mary were set up in his stead, Penn was very much suspected of wishing to bring James back. He was arrested several times, but nothing could be proved against him. The control of Pennsylvania was taken from him also, but this was afterwards restored.

Penn returned to Pennsylvania in 1699. He was once taking a journey through his province when he met a little girl named Rebecca Wood going to "meeting" on foot. He took the little girl up behind him on his horse, and the great proprietor of Pennsylvania was seen riding gravely along with the bare legs and feet of a poor little girl dangling at his horse's side.

Penn returned again to England, and, after many years, died in 1718. His descendants appointed the governors of Pennsylvania until the Revolution.

King Philip

When the Pilgrims first came to New England they found that the nearest tribe of Indians, the Wam-pa-no'-ags, of which Massasoit was chief, had been much reduced in number by a dreadful sickness. The bones of the dead lay bleaching on the ground.

The next neighbors to the Wampanoags were the Narragansetts. These had not been visited by the great sickness, but were as numerous and strong as ever. Massasoit was, therefore, very glad to have the English, with their strange guns and long swords, near him, to protect his people from the Narragansetts.

The two sons of Massasoit had been named by the white people Alexander and Philip, and they were very proud of their names. These young men remained friendly to the settlers for some time after their father's death. But many things made the Indians discontented. They readily sold their lands to the white people for blankets, hatchets, toys, and such things. The ground was all covered with woods, and, as they used it only for hunting, it was of little value. But when they saw how much the white men made out of it they wished to be paid over again.

Many of this tribe of Indians became Christians through the preaching of John Eliot, who was called "The Apostle to the Indians." These were called "praying Indians." They settled in villages and tried to live like white people, though they continued to dwell in bark houses, because they found that the easiest way to clean house was to leave the old one and built a new one. They no longer followed their chiefs or respected the charms of the medicine men. It made the great men among the Indians angry to see their people leave them.

The young chief Alexander began to show ill feeling toward the white people. The rulers of Plymouth Colony took harsh measures with him. They sent some soldiers and brought him to Plymouth to answer for his conduct. When this proud Indian saw himself arrested and degraded in this way he felt it bitterly. He was taken sick at Plymouth, and died soon after he got home.

The Indians imagined that Alexander had died of poison given him by white men. Some time afterwards the white people heard that Alexander's brother, Philip, was sharpening hatchets and knives. They immediately sent for him, and forced him and his men to give up the seventy guns they had brought with them. They also made Philip promise to send in all the other guns his men had.

When the white people first came, the Indians had nothing to shoot with but bows and arrows. In Philip's time they had given up bows, finding guns much better for killing game. You may be sure that when Philip once got away from the white people he did not send in any more guns. But he hid his anger, as an Indian always does, and waited for a chance to strike.

Though Philip lived in a common, dirty wigwam, and was probably often in need of food, he was called King Philip, and he proudly called himself a king and thought himself as great a man as the King of England. He had a coat made of shell beads, or wampum. These beads were made by breaking and polishing little bits of hard-clam shells, and then boring a hole through them with a stone awl, as you see in the picture. Wampum was used for money among the Indians, and even among the white people at that time. Such a coat as Philip's was very valuable. Philip dressed himself, also, in a showy red blanket; he wore a belt of wampum about his head and another long belt of wampum around his neck, the ends of which dangled nearly to the ground.

The quarrel between the white people and the Indians grew more bitter. An Indian, who had told the white men of Philip's plans, was put to death, probably by Philip's order. The white people hanged the Indians who had killed their friend.

The Indians under Philip were now resolved on war. But their medicine men, or priests, who pretended to talk with spirits, told them that whichever side should shed the first blood would be beaten in the war. The Indians burned houses and robbed farms, but they took pains not to kill anybody, until a white man had wounded an Indian. Then, when blood had been shed, they began to kill the white people.

This Indian war broke out in 1675. The New England people lived at that time in villages, most of them not very far from the sea. The more exposed towns were struck first. The people took refuge in strong houses, which were built to resist the Indians. But everywhere those who moved about were killed. Some were shot in going for water, others were slain as they ran out after the savages had set fire to their houses.

The white men sent out troops, but the Indians sometimes waylaid soldiers and killed them suddenly. Philip cut up his fine wampum coat and sent the bead money of which it was made to neighboring chiefs to persuade them to join him. Soon other tribes, anxious to share in the plunder and slaughter, entered the fight.

As the Indians grew bolder, they attacked the white men in their forts or blockhouses. At Brookfield they shot burning arrow son the roof of the blockhouse, but the white men tore off the shingles and put out the fire. Then the savages crept up and lighted a fire under one corner of the house; but the men inside made a dash and drove back the enemy and put the fire out. Then the Indians made a cart with a barrel for a wheel. They loaded this with straw and lighted it, and backed the blazing mass up against the house, sheltering themselves behind it. Luckily a shower came up at that moment and put out the fire.

A very curious thing happened at Hadley. An old gentleman named General Goffe was hid away in a house in that town. He was one of the judges that had condemned Charles I to death twenty-six years before. When the son of King Charles I came to be king he put to death such of these judges as he could find, and Goffe had to flee from England and hide. Nobody in the village knew that Goffe was there, except those who entertained him. While all the people were at church one Sunday, the old general ventured to look out of the window, which he did not dare to do at other times. He saw the Indians coming to attack the town. He rushed out and gave the alarm, and, with long white hair and beard streaming in the wind, the old soldier took command of the villagers, who soon drove back the savages. But when the fight was over, the people could not find the old man who had led them, nor did they know who he was or where he came from. They said that a messenger had been sent from heaven to deliver them.

The powerful tribe of the Narragansetts promised to remain peaceable, but young savages are too fond of war to miss a chance to engage in a battle. Some of the Narragansetts joined Philip, and their great fort was a refuge for Philip's men. They were probably waiting for spring to come before openly joining in the war.

The white men resolved to strike the first blow against them while it was yet winter. A thousand men from Massachusetts and Connecticut pushed through the snow and made a desperate assault by night on the Narragansett town, which was inside a fortification having but one entrance, and that by a bridge. Nearly two hundred of the white men were killed in this fight, and many hundreds of Indians were slain, and their fort and all their provisions were burned. The white men marched back, carrying their wounded through the bitter cold.

The Narragansetts took a terrible revenge. They joined Philip at once. Towns were now burned and people killed in every direction. The white men in armor could not catch the nimble Indians, who massacred the people in one village only to disappear and strike another village far away. Many women and children were carried into captivity by the Indians.

Captain Church in Philip's War

The white men had not learned how to fight the Indians, who moved swiftly from place to place, and hid themselves in the darkest swamps. But at last the man was found who could battle with the Indians in their own way. This was Captain Benjamin Church.

Church could not only fight the Indians, but he knew how to make them his friends. One tribe, not far from his home, was under the control of a squaw sachem, or woman chief. Her name was Awashonks. She and Benjamin Church were good friends, and after the war broke out Church tried to go to see her, but some of the Indians of her tribe who were friendly to Philip attacked Church and his men, so that they had to hide behind a fence till a boat came and took them away.

Later in the war, church sent word to Awashonks that he would meet her and four other Indians at a certain place. But the rulers of Plymouth Colony thought it too dangerous for church to go to see the squaw sachem. They would not give him any men for such an expedition.

However, Church went on his own account, with one white man and three Indians. He took some tobacco and a bottle of rum as presents suited to the taste of this Indian queen. Church ventured ashore, leaving his canoe to stand off at a safe distance, so that if he should be killed the men in the canoe might carry the news to the white people. Awashonks and the four Indians met him and thanked him for venturing among them. But soon a great number of warriors, frightfully painted and armed, rose up out of the tall grass and surrounded Captain church. The captain knew that if he showed himself frightened he would be killed.

"Have you not met me to talk about peace?" he said to Awashonks.

"Yes," said Awashonks.

"When people meet to talk of peace they lay down their arms," said Captain Church.

The Indians now began to look surly and to mutter something.

"If you will put aside your guns, that will do," said Church.

The Indian warriors laid down their guns and squatted on the grass. During the discussion some of them grew angry, and one fellow with a wooden tomahawk wished to kill Church, but the others pushed him away. The captain succeeded in making peace with this tribe, who agreed to take the side of the English against Philip.

Awashonks held a war dance after this, and Church attended. The Indians lighted a great bonfire, and moved about it in rings. One of the braves stepped inside the circle and called out the name of one of the tribes fighting on Philip's side against the white people. Then he pulled a firebrand out of the fire to represent that tribe, and he made a show of fighting with the firebrand. Every time the name of a tribe was called, a firebrand was drawn out and attacked in this way.

After this ceremony Church could call on as many of these Indians as he wished to help him against Philip. With small bands of these Indians and a few white men Captain Church scoured the woods, capturing a great many Indian prisoners.

From the prisoners that he took, Church chose certain ones and made them soldiers under him. He would say to one of these men: "Come! come! You look wild, and mutter. That doesn't matter. The best soldiers I have got were as wild and surly as you a little while ago. By the time you've been one day with me you'll love me, too, and be as active as any of them."

And it always turned out so. The captain was so jolly, and yet so bold and so successful, that the savage whom he chose to help him would presently do anything for him, even to capturing his own friends.

At last so many of Philip's Indians were taken that Philip himself was fleeing from swamp to swamp to avoid falling into the hands of the white men. But he grew fiercer as he grew more desperate. He killed one of his men for telling him that he ought to make peace with the white men. The brother of the man whom he killed ran away from Philip, and came into the settlement to tell the white people where to find that chief.

Captain Church had just come from chasing Philip to make a short visit to his wife. The poor woman had been so anxious for her husband's safety that she fainted when she saw him. By the time she had recovered the Indian deserter came to tell Church where Philip could be found, and the captain galloped off at once.

Church placed his men near the swamp in which Philip was hidden. The Indians took the alarm and fled. In running away Philip ran straight toward Church's hidden men, and was shot by the very Indian whose brother he had killed. His head was cut off and stuck up over a gatepost at Plymouth. Such was the ugly custom in that day.

Philip's chief captain, Annawon, got away with a considerable number of Indians. Church and half a dozen of his Indian scouts captured an old Indian and a young squaw who belonged to Annawon's party. They made these two walk ahead of them carrying baskets, while Church and his men crept behind them. In this way they got down a steep bank right into the camp of

Annawon, whose party was much stronger than Church's. But Church boldly seized the guns of the Indians, which were stacked together.

"I am taken," cried Annawon.

"What have you got for supper?" asked Church. "I have come to sup with you."

Annawon ordered the women to hurry up supper, and when it was ready he asked Church whether he would have "horse beef" or "cow beef." Church preferred to eat cow beef.

The captain told his Indians to stand guard while he tried to get a nap. But soon all were fast asleep except Church and Annawon, who lay eying each other. Presently, Annawon got up and walked away. Church moved all the Indians' guns close to himself. He thought that the old chief might have gone for another gun, and he lay down beside the chief's son, so that Annawon could not shoot him without killing his own son.

But Annawon came back with a bundle in his arms. He fell on his knees before Church.

"Great captain," he said, "you have killed Philip and conquered his country. I and my company are the last. This war is ended by you, and therefore these things are yours."

He opened the bundle, which contained Philip's belts of wampum and the red blanket in which Philip dressed on great occasions.

This ended King Philip's War.

Bacon and His Men

In 1676, just a hundred years before the American Revolution, the people of Virginia were very much oppressed by Sir William Berkeley, the governor appointed by the King of England. Their property was taken away by unjust taxes, and in other ways. The governor had managed to get all the power into his own hands and those of his friends.

This was the time of King Philip's War in New England. The news of this war made the Indians of Virginia uneasy, and at length the Susquehannas and other tribes attacked the frontiers. Governor Berkeley would not do anything to protect the people on the frontier, because he was making a great deal of money out of the trade with friendly Indians, and if troops were sent against them this trade would be stopped.

When many hundreds of people on the frontier had been put to death, some three hundred men formed themselves into a company to punish the Indians. But Berkeley refused to allow any one to take command of this troop, or to let them go against the savages.

There was a brilliant young gentleman named Nathaniel Bacon, who had come from England three years before. He was a member of the governor's Council, and an educated man of wealth. He begged the governor to let him lead this company of three hundred men against the Indians; but the cruel and stubborn old governor said, No.

Bacon was sorry for the suffering people. He went to the camp of these men, to see and encourage them. But when they saw him they set up the cry, "A Bacon! A Bacon! A Bacon!" This was the way of cheering a man at that day and choosing him for a leader.

Bacon knew that the governor might put him to death if he disobeyed orders, but he could not refuse these poor men who had been driven from their homes. So off he went at their head to the Indian towns, where he killed many of the savages.

The old governor gathered his friends and started after Bacon, declaring that he would hang him for going to war without orders; but while he was looking for him, the people down by the coast rose in favor of Bacon. The governor had to make peace with them by promising to let them choose a new Legislature.

When Bacon got back from the Indian country the frontier people nearly worshiped him as their deliverer. They kept guard night and day over his house. They were afraid the angry governor would send men to kill him.

The people of his county elected Bacon a member of the new Legislature. But they were afraid the governor might harm him. Forty of them with guns went down to Jamestown with him in a sloop. With the help of two boats and a ship the governor captured Bacon's sloop, and brought Bacon into Jamestown. But as the angry people were already rising to defend their leader, Berkeley was afraid to hurt him. He made him apologize, and restored him to his place in the Council.

But that night Bacon was warned that the next day he would be seized again, and that the roads and river were guarded to keep him from getting away. So he took horse suddenly and galloped out of Jamestown in the darkness. The next morning the governor sent men to search the house where he had stayed. They stuck their swords through the beds, thinking him hidden there.

But Bacon was already among friends. When the country people heard that he was in danger, they seized their guns and vowed to kill the governor and all his party. Bacon was quickly marching on Jamestown with five hundred angry men at his back. The people refused to help the governor, and Bacon and his men entered Jamestown. It was their turn to guard the roads and keep Berkeley in.

The old governor offered to fight the young captain single-handed, but Bacon told him he would not harm him. Bacon forced the governor to sign a commission appointing him a general. He also made the Legislature pass good laws for the relief of the people. These laws were remembered long after Nathaniel Bacon's death, and were known as "Bacon's Laws."

While this work of doing away with bad laws and making good ones was going on, the Indians crept down to a place only about twenty miles from Jamestown and murdered the people. General Bacon promptly started for the Indian country with his little army. But, just as he was leaving the settlements, he heard that the governor was raising troops to take him when he should get back; so he turned about and marched swiftly back to Jamestown.

The governor had called out the militia, but when they learned that instead of taking them to fight the Indians they were to go against Bacon, they all began to murder "Bacon! Bacon! Bacon!" Then they left the field and went home, and the old governor fainted with disappointment. He was forced to flee for safety to the eastern shore of Chesapeake Bay, and the government fell into the hands of General Bacon.

Bacon had an enemy on each side of him. No sooner had Berkeley gone than the Indians again began their murders. Bacon once more marched against them, and killed many. He and his men lived on horseflesh and chinquapin nuts during this expedition.

When Bacon got back to the settlements and had dismissed all but one hundred and thirty-six of his men, he heard that Governor Berkeley had gathered together seventeen little vessels and six hundred sailors and others, and with these had taken possession of Jamestown. Worn out as they were with fatigue and hunger, Bacon persuaded his little band to march straight for Jamestown, so as to take Berkeley by surprise.

As the weary and dusty heroes of the Indian war hurried onward to Jamestown, the people cheered the gallant little company. The women called after Bacon, "General, if you need help, send for us!" So fast did these men march that they reached the narrow neck of sand that connected Jamestown with the mainland before the governor had heard of their coming. Bacon's men dug trenches in the night, and shut in the governor and his people.

After a while Bacon got some cannon. He wanted to put them upon his breastworks without losing the life of any of his brave soldiers. So he sent to the plantations near by and brought to his camp the wives of the chief men in the governor's party. These ladies he made to sit down in front of his works until his cannon were in place. He knew that the enemy would not fire on them. When he had finished, he politely sent them home.

Great numbers of the people now flocked to General Bacon's standard, and the governor and his followers left Jamestown in their vessels. Knowing that they would try to return, Bacon ordered the town to be burned to the ground.

Almost all of the people except those on the eastern shore sided with Bacon, who now did his best to put the government in order. But the hardships he had been through were too much for him. He sickened and died. His friends knew that Berkeley would soon get control again, now that their leader was dead. They knew that his enemies would dig up Bacon's body and hang it, after the fashion of that time. Therefore they buried it nobody knows where; but as they put stones into his coffin, they must have sunk it in the river.

Governor Berkeley got back his power, and hanged many of Bacon's friends. But the King of England removed Berkeley in disgrace, and he died of a broken heart. The governors who came after were generally careful not to oppress the people too far. They were afraid another Bacon might rise up against them.

Boyhood of Franklin

Benjamin Franklin, the fifteenth in a family of seventeen children, was born in Boston in 1706. Benjamin learned to read when he was very young, but he was sent to school for only two years. When he was ten years old he had to help his father. Franklin's father made his living by boiling soap and making tallow candles. Little Benjamin had to cut wicks for the candles, fill the molds with the melted tallow, tend the shop, and run on errands. He did not like the soap and candle trade. Playing about the water, he had learned to swim, and to manage a boat, when he was very young. Like many other boys, he got the notion that it would be a fine thing to go to sea and be a sailor. But his father did not think so.

Franklin and his playmates used to fish for minnows in a mill pond which had a salt marsh for a shore, so that the boys had to stand in the mud. He was a leader among the boys, and already very ingenious. So he proposed that the boys should build a little wharf in this marsh to stand on. Near the marsh there was a pile of stones, put there to be used in building a new house. In the evening, when the workmen were gone, Franklin and the other boys tugged and toiled until they had managed to carry all these stones away and build them into a wharf, or pier, reaching out into the water.

In the morning the workmen were very much surprised to find that their pile of stones had walked away during the night. They soon found out where the stones were, and complained to the parents of the boys. Franklin and some of the other boys were punished for their mischief. Benjamin tried to make his father see that it was a very useful work to build such a pier, but the father soon showed him that "nothing was useful that was not honest."

When Franklin had worked for two years with the father at the trade of making tallow candles, the father began to be afraid that Ben would run away and go to sea, as another of his sons had done before. So Franklin's father took him to walk with him sometimes, showing him men working at their trades, such as bricklaying, turning, and joining, hoping that the boy would take a fancy to one of these occupations. Meantime, Benjamin became very fond of reading. He read his father's books, which were very dull for children, and he sold some little things of his own to buy more. As the boy was so fond of books, Benjamin's father could think of nothing better than to make him a printer. So Benjamin was apprenticed to his older brother, James Franklin, who already had a printing office. Benjamin liked this trade, and learned very fast. As he was often sent to bookstores, he got a chance to borrow books. He sometimes sat up all night to read one of these, taking great care to keep the books clean and to return them soon.

Benjamin took a fancy to write poetry about this time. His brother printed this "wretched stuff," as Franklin afterwards called it, and sent the boy around the town to peddle it. Ben was very proud of his poetry until his father made fun of it, and told him that "verse-makers were generally beggars."

Franklin had a notion as a boy that it was wrong to eat meat, so he told his brother that if he would give him half of what his board cost, he would board himself. After this, Benjamin made his dinner on biscuit or a tart from the baker's. In this way he saved some of his board money to buy books, and used the time while the other printers were at dinner to study.

James Franklin, Benjamin's brother, printed a little newspaper. Franklin was printer's boy and paper carrier, for after he had worked at printing the papers, he carried them around to the houses of the subscribers. But he also wanted to write for the paper. He did not dare propose to bold a thing to his brother, so he wrote some articles and put them under the printing-office door at night. They were printed, and even Benjamin's brother did not suspect that they were written by the boy.

The two brothers did not get on well together. The younger brother was rather saucy, and the older brother, who was high-tempered, sometimes gave him a whipping.

James Franklin once printed something in his newspaper which offended the government of the colony. He was arrested and put into prison for a month; for the press was not free in that day. Benjamin published the paper while his brother was in prison, and put in the sharpest things he dared to say about the government. After James got out of prison he was forbidden to print a newspaper any longer. So he made up his mind to print it in the name of his brother Benjamin. In order to do this he was obliged to release Benjamin Franklin from his apprenticeship, though it was agreed that Ben was to remain at work for his brother, as though still an apprentice, till he was twenty-one years old. But Benjamin soon got into another quarrel with his brother James, and, now that he was no longer bound, he left him. This was not fair on his part, and he was afterwards sorry for it.

Franklin, The Printer

When Ben Franklin left his brother he tried in vain to get a place in one of the other printing offices in Boston. But James Franklin had sent word to the other printers not to take Benjamin into their employ. There was no other town nearer than New York large enough to support a printing office. Franklin, who was now but seventeen years old, sold some of his books, and secretly got aboard a sloop ready to sail to New York. In New York he could find no work, but was recommended to try in Philadelphia.

The modes of travel in that time were very rough. The easiest way of getting from Boston to New York was by sailing vessels. To get to Philadelphia, Franklin had first to take a sailboat to Amboy, in New Jersey. On the way a squall of wind tore the sails and drove the boat to anchor near the Long Island shore, where our runaway boy lay all night in the little hold of the boat, with the waves beating over the deck and the water leaking down on him. When at last he landed at Amboy, he had been thirty hours without anything to eat or any water to drink.

Having but little money in his pocket, he had to walk from Amboy to Burlington; and when, soaked with rain, he stopped at an inn, he cut such a figure that the people came near arresting him for a runaway bond servant, of whom there were many at that time. He thought he might better have stayed at home.

This tired and mud-bespattered young fellow got a chance to go from Burlington to Philadelphia in a rowboat by taking his turn at the oars. There were no street lamps in the town of Philadelphia, and the men in the boat passed the town without knowing it. Like forlorn tramps, they landed and made a fire of some fence rails.

When they got back to Philadelphia in the morning, Franklin—who was to become in time the most famous man in that town—walked up the street in his working clothes, which were badly soiled by his rough journey. His spare stockings and shirt were stuffed into his pockets.

He bought three large rolls at a baker's shop. One of these he carried under each arm; the other he munched as he walked.

As he passed along the street a girl named Deborah Read stood in the door of her father's house, and laughed at the funny sight of a young fellow with bulging pockets and a roll under each arm. Years afterwards this same Deborah was married to Franklin.

Franklin got a place to work with a printer named Keimer. He was now only a poor printer-boy, in leather breeches such as workingmen wore at that time. But, though he looked poor, he was already different from most of the boys in Philadelphia. He was a lover of good books. The boy who has learned to read the best books will be an educated man, with or without schools. The great difference between people is shown in the way they spend their leisure time. Franklin, when not studying, spent his evenings with a few young men who were also fond of books. Here is the sort of young man that will come to something.

I suppose people began to notice and talk about this studious young workman. One day Keimer, the printer for whom Franklin was at work, saw, coming toward his office, Sir William Keith, the governor of the province of Pennsylvania, and another gentleman, both finely dressed after the fashion of the time, in powdered periwigs and silver knee buckles. Keimer was delighted to have such visitors, and he ran down to meet the great men. But imagine his disappointment when the governor asked to see Franklin, and led away the young printer in leather breeches to talk with him in the tavern.

The governor wanted Franklin to set up a printing office of his own, because both Keimer and the other master printer in Philadelphia were poor workmen. But Franklin had no money, and it took a great deal to buy a printing press and types in that day. Franklin told the governor that he did not believe his father would help him to buy an outfit. But the governor wrote a letter himself to Franklin's father, asking him to start Benjamin in business.

So Franklin went back to Boston in a better plight than that in which he had left. He had on a brand new suit of clothes, he carried a watch, and he had some silver in his pockets. His father and mother were glad to see him once more, but his father told him he was too young to start in business for himself.

Franklin returned to Philadelphia, Governor Keith, who was one of those fine gentlemen that make many promising speeches, now offered to start Franklin himself. He wanted him to go to London to buy the printing press.

He promised to give the young man letters to people in London, and one that would get him the money to buy the press.

But, somehow, every time that Franklin called on the governor for the letters he was told to call again. At last Franklin went on shipboard, thinking the governor had sent the letters in the ship's letter bag. Before the ship got to England the bag was opened, and no letters for Franklin were found. A gentleman now told Franklin that Keith made a great many such promises, but he never kept them. Fine clothes do not make a fine gentleman.

So Franklin was left in London without money or friends. But he got work as a printer, and learned some things about the business that he could not learn in America. The English printers drank a great deal of beer. They laughed at Franklin because he did not drink beer, and they called him the "Water American." But he wasn't a fellow to be afraid of ridicule. They told him that water would make him weak, but they were surprised to find him able to lift more than any of them. He was also the strongest and most expert swimmer of all. In London he kept up his reading. He paid a man who kept a secondhand bookstore for permission to read his books.

Franklin came back to Philadelphia as clerk for a merchant; but the merchant soon died, and Franklin went to work again for his old master, Keimer. He was very useful, for he could make ink and cast type when they were needed, and he also engraved some designs on type metal. Keimer once fell out with Franklin, and discharged him; but he begged him to come back when there was some paper money to be printed, with Keimer could not print without Franklin's help in making the engravings.

The Great Doctor Franklin

After a time Franklin started a printing office of his own. He was very much in debt for his printing press and types. To pay for them he worked very hard. Men saw him at work when they got up in the morning, and when they went to bed at night the candle in his office was still shining. When he wanted paper he would sometimes take the wheelbarrow himself and bring it from the store at which he bought it to his printing office.

People began to say: "What an honest, hard-working young man that Franklin is! He is sure to get on!" And then, to help him get on, they brought their work to his office.

He started a newspaper. Now his reading of good books and his practice in writing since he was a little boy helped him. He could write intelligently on almost any subject, and his paper was the best one printed in all America at that time.

Franklin married Miss Deborah Read, the same who had laughed when she saw him walking the street with a roll under each arm and his spare clothes in his pockets. His wife helped him to attend the shop, for he sold stationery in connection with his printing. They kept no servant, and Franklin ate his breakfast of plain bread and milk out of an earthen porringer with a pewter spoon. In time he paid off all his debts and began to grow rich.

In those days books were scarce and people had but few of them. But everybody bought an almanac. Franklin published one of these useful little pamphlets every year. It was known as "Poor Richard's Almanac," because it pretended to be written by a poor man named Richard Saunders, though everybody knew that Richard was Franklin himself. This almanac was very popular on account of the wise and witty sayings of Poor Richard about saving time and money.

Franklin did not spend all his time making money. He studied hard as usual, and succeeded in learning several languages without the help of a teacher. This knowledge was afterwards of the greatest use to him.

Like other people in America at that time, he found it hard to get the books he wanted. To help himself and to do good to others, he started a public library in Philadelphia, which was the first ever started in America. Many like it were established in other towns, and the people in America soon had books within their reach. It was observed, after a while, that plain people in America knew more than people in the same circumstances in other countries.

Franklin did many other things for the public. Seeing how wasteful the old fireplaces were, since they burned a great deal of wood and made the rooms cold and full of draughts, and often filled the house with smoke, he invented a system of saving heat by means of a small iron fireplace or open stove. He founded a high school, which afterwards became a great university. When the frontier people were slai8n by Indians during the French War, he was the chief man in raising and arming troops for their relief.

These and other acts of the sort made Franklin well known in Pennsylvania. But he presently did one thing which made him famous all the world over. This one thing was accomplished in a very short time; but it came from the habits of study he formed when he was a little boy. He was always reading, to get more knowledge, and making experiments, to find out things. People did not know a great deal about electricity at that time. In Europe many learned men were trying to find out what they could about various sorts of electricity, and lectures on the subject had been given in Philadelphia. Something made Franklin think that the electricity which was produced by a machine was of the same nature as the lightning in the sky. So he devised a plan to find out. He set a trap to catch the lightning. He made a kite by stretching a silk handkerchief on a frame. Then he fastened a metal point to the kite and tied a hemp string to it to fly it with. He thought that if lightning were electricity, it would go from the metal point down the hemp string. At the lower end of the string he tied a key, and a silk string to catch hold of, so that he should not let the electricity escape though his hand.

Franklin knew that if a grown man were seen flying a kite he would soon be surrounded by a crowd. So one stormy night he went out and sent up his kite. He waited under a shed to see if the electricity would come. When he saw the little fibers of the hemp stand up charged with electricity, he held his hand near the key and felt a shock. Then he went home, the only man in the world that knew certainly that lightning was electricity. When he had found out this secret he invented the lightning rod, which takes electricity from the air to the earth and keeps it from doing harm.

When the learned men of Europe heard that a man who had hardly ever been at school had made a great discovery, they were struck with wonder, and Franklin was soon considered one of the great men of the world, and was called Dr. Franklin.

When the troubles between England and her colonies began, there was no one so suitable to make peace as the famous Dr. Franklin. Franklin went to

England and tried hard to settle matters. But he would not consent to any plan by which Americans should give up their rights.

When the war broke out Dr. Franklin came home again. He was made a member of Congress, and he helped to make the Declaration of Independence. After the Americans had declared themselves independent they found it a hard task to fight against so powerful a country as England. They wanted to get some other country to help them. So Franklin, who was well known in Europe, and who had studied French when he was a poor printer, was sent to France.

When Franklin went to France he had to appear at the finest court in the world. But in the midst of all the display and luxury of the French court he wore plain clothes, and did not pretend to be anything more than he was in Philadelphia. This pleased the French, who admired his independent spirit and called him "the philosopher." He persuaded the French Government to give money and arms to the Americans. He fitted out vessels to attack English ships, and during the whole War of the Revolution he did much for his country.

When the war was ended there came the hard task of making peace. In this Franklin took a leading part.

When peace had been made, Dr. Franklin set out to leave Paris. As he was old and feeble, the queen's litter, which was carried by mules, was furnished to him. On this litter he traveled till he reached the sea. After he got home he was the most honored man in America next to Washington. He became a member of the Convention of 1787, which formed the Constitution of the United States. He died in 1790, at the age of eighty-four.

When Franklin was a boy his father used to repeat to him Solomon's proverb, "Seest thou a man diligent in his business? he shall stand before kings." This was always an encouragement to him, though he did not expect really to stand before kings. But he was presented to five different kings in his lifetime.

Young George Washington

George washington was born in a plain, old-fashioned house in Westmoreland Country, Virginia, on the twenty-second day of February, 1732. He was sent to what was called an "old-field school." The country schoolhouses in Virginia at that time were built in fields too much worn out to grow anything. Little George Washington went to a school taught by a man named Hobby.

In that day the land in Virginia was left to the oldest son, after the custom in England, for Virginia was an English colony. As George's elder brother Lawrence was to have the land and be the great gentleman of the family, he had been sent to England for his education. When he got back, with many a strange story of England to tell, George became very proud of him, and Lawrence was equally pleased with his manly little brother. When Lawrence went away as a captain, in the regiment raised in America for service in the English army against the Spaniards in the West Indies, George began to think much of a soldier's life, and to drill the boys in Hobby's school. There were marches and parades and bloodless battles fought among the tufts of broom straw in the old field, and in these young George was captain.

This play-captain soon came to be a tall boy. He could run swiftly, and he was a powerful wrestler. The stories of the long jumps he made are almost beyond belief. It was also said that he could throw farther than anybody else. The people of that day went everywhere on horseback, and George was not afraid to get astride of the wildest horse or an unbroken colt. These things proved that he was a strongly built and fearless boy. But a better thing is told of him. He was so just, that his schoolmates used to bring their quarrels for him to settle.

When Washington was eleven years old his father died, but this mother took pains to bring him up with manly ideas. He was now sent to school to a Mr. Williams, from whom he learned reading, writing, and arithmetic. To these were added a little bookkeeping and surveying.

George took great pains with all he did. His copybooks have been kept, and they show that his handwriting was very neat. He also wrote out over one hundred "rules for behavior in company." You see that he wished to be a gentleman in every way.

His brother Lawrence wished George to learn to be a seaman, and George himself like the notion of going to sea. But his mother was unwilling to part with him. So he stayed at school until he was sixteen years old.

A great deal of the northern part of Virginia at this time belonged to Lord Fairfax, an eccentric nobleman, whose estates included many whole counties. George Washington must have studied his books of surveying very carefully, for he was only a large boy when he was employed to go over beyond the Blue Ridge Mountains and survey some of the wild lands of Lord Fairfax.

So, when he was just sixteen years old, young Washington accepted the offer of Lord Fairfax, and set out for the wilderness. He crossed rough mountains and rode his horse through swollen streams. The settlers' beds were only masses of straw, with, perhaps, a ragged blanket. But George slept most of the time out under the sky by a camp fire, with a little hay, straw, or fodder for a bed. Sometimes men and women and children slept around these fires, "like cats and dogs," as Washington wrote, "and happy is he who gets nearest the fire." Once the straw on which the young surveyor was asleep blazed up, and he might have been consumed if one of the party had not waked him in time. Washington must have been a pretty good surveyor, for he received large pay for his work, earning from seven to twenty-one dollars a day, at a time when things were much cheaper than they are now.

The food of people in the woods was the flesh of wild turkey and other game. Every man was his own cook, toasting his meat on a forked stick, and eating it off a chip instead of a plate. Washington led this rough life for three years. It was a good school for a soldier. Here, too, he made his first acquaintance with the Indians. He saw a party of them dance to the music of a drum made by stretching deerskin very tight over the top of a pot half full of water. They also had a rattle, made by putting shot into a gourd. They took pains to tie a piece of a horse's tail to the gourd, so as to see the horsehair switch to and fro when the gourd was shaken.

When Washington was but nineteen years old the governor of Virginia made him a major of militia. He took lessons in military drill from an old soldier, and practiced sword exercises under the instruction of a Dutchman named Van Braam. The people in Virginia and the other colonies were looking forward to a war with the French, who in that day had colonies in Canada and Louisiana. They claimed the country west of the Alleghany Mountains. The English colonists had spread over most of the country east of the mountains, and they were beginning to cross the Alleghanies. But the French built forts on the west side of the mountains, and stirred up the

Indians to prevent the English settlers from coming over into the rich valley of the Ohio River.

The governor of Virginia resolved to send an officer to warn the French that they were on English ground. Who was so fit to go on this hard and dangerous errand as the brave young Major Washington, who knew both the woods and the ways of the Indians? So Washington set out with a few hardy frontiersmen. When at length, after crossing swollen streams and rough mountains, he got over to the Ohio River, where all was wilderness, he called the Indians together and had a big talk with them, at a place called Logtown. He got a chief called "The Half-king," and some other Indians, to go with him to the French fort.

The French officers had no notion of giving up their fort to the English. They liked this brave and gentlemanly young Major Washington, and entertained him well. But they tried to get the Half-king and his Indians to leave Washington, and did what they could to keep him from getting safe home again. With a great deal of trouble he got his Indians away from the French fort at last, and started back. Part of the way they traveled in canoes, jumping out into the icy water now and then to life the canoes over shallow places.

When Washington came to the place where he was to leave the Indians and recross the mountains, his pack horses were found to be so weak that they were unfit for their work. So Major Washington gave up his saddle horse to carry the baggage. Then he strapped a pack on his back, shouldered his gun, and with a man named Gist set out ahead of the rest of the party.

Washington and Gist had a rascally Indian for guide. When Washington was tired this fellow wished to carry his gun for him, but the young major thought the gun safer in his own hands. At length, as evening came on, the Indian turned suddenly, leveled his gun, and fired on Washington and Gist, in the dark, but without hitting either of them. They seized him before he could reload his gun. Gist wanted to kill him, but Washington thought it better to let him go.

Afraid of being attacked, they now traveled night and day till they got to the Allegheny River. This was full of floating ice, and they tried to cross it on a raft. Washington was pushing the raft with a pole, when the ice caught the pole in such a way as to fling him into the river. He caught hold of the raft and got out again. He and Gist spent the cold night on an island in the river, and got ashore in the morning by walking on the ice.

They now stopped at the house of an Indian trader. Near by was s squaw chief, who was offended that she had not been asked to the council

Washington had held with the Indians at Logtown. To make friends, he paid her a visit, and presented her with a blanket such as the Indians wear on their shoulders. Washington bought a horse here, and soon got back to the settlements, where the story of the adventures of the young major was told from one plantation to another, producing much excitement.

Washington in the French War

When Washington got back from the western side of the mountains, it became evident to the governor of Virginia that the French must be either driven away or the English people must be shut in to the country on the east of the Mountains. The people in the colonies did not like the notion of being fenced in like a lot of cattle in a pasture. So Washington was again sent to the West in 1754, to take possession of the country. On his first trip he had seen the point where the Allegheny and Monongahela rivers meet, which he thought would be a good place for a fort. A small company of men were sent ahead to build a fort at this place; but the French drove them away, and planted a fort of their own on the ground. This was called Fort Duquesne.

Though the French in America were not many, they were nearly all soldiers. So when Washington with his party had got through the wild mountains into the western wilderness he found that there were many more soldiers on the French side than he had. Hearing that a French party was dogging his steps, he marched in the night and surrounded them. After a sharp skirmish the French fled, but were nearly all captured. This little fight was George Washington's first battle.

But Washington soon found that he must retreat or be taken. He fell back to a place called Great Meadows, where he built a sort of fort and called it Fort Necessity. Here the Half-king in despair left him, and the French attacked his little force. After the conflict had lasted one day, Washington, seeing himself outnumbered, agreed to march out of the fort and return to the settlements, which he did. This expedition of Washington's was the beginning of a great war between England and France.

The next year troops were sent from England under General Braddock, who set out to drive the French from Fort Duquesne. Braddock was a brave man, but one of the sort who can not learn anything. He laughed at the lank and careless-looking American troops, who cut a sorry figure alongside of the English with their bright red coats and fine drill. He was sure that these rough Americans were of no use. Even American officers were treated with contempt by the British authorities, and were not allowed to rank with English officers. Washington was so stung by this that he resigned his place, but he accepted a position on Braddock's staff.

Rough as the mountain roads were, Braddock traveled in a coach as far as he could, and tried to keep up the display common in Europe. He said that the Indians would not prove formidable when they came to fight his well-drilled English troops. Washington could not persuade the general to send scouts on either side of his line. One day there came to Braddock a company of woodsmen in hunting shirts. They were commanded by the famous Captain Jack, who was known as the "Black Hunter" of Pennsylvania. Captain Jack's whole family had been killed by the savages in his absence. He had then taken to the woods, and devoted himself to revenging the death of his family and to protecting the settlers. He and his followers lived in the forest, and kept the Indians in constant fear of them. This Captain Jack, and all his men, came to General Braddock and offered to help him as scouts. But Braddock put all his confidence in his solid ranks of English soldiers, and he foolishly refused the offer of the Black Hunter and his men.

As the army drew near to Fort Duquesne, Washington suggested to the commander that the Virginia rangers should be sent in front, because they were used to the woods. But Braddock was angry to think that a young American should advise an old British general.

On the 9th of July, 1755, as Braddock's army was marching along the narrow track through the woods, the Indians and French attacked them. All at once the woods rang with the wild war cry of the Indians, like the barking of a thousand wild animals. The forest, but a minute before so silent, was alive with screaming savages. From every tree and thicket the Indians leveled their rifles at the red coats of the English, who fell like pigeons under their fire. Unable to see anybody to shoot at, the English soldiers did not know what to do. The Americans took to the trees and stumps and returned the fire in Indian fashion, and Washington begged the general to order the British to do the same; but Braddock made them stand up in line, where they could easily be shot down.

Braddock fought bravely, and fell at length mortally wounded. Colonel Washington did his best to rally the men and save the battle. He had two horses shot under him, and four bullets went through his coat. The army, so gay and brave in the morning, was soon broken to pieces, and the men fled back to the settlements.

But Washington had become the hero of the people. He was now put in chief command of the Virginia troops in defense of the frontier, and managed affairs well. In 1758 he commanded the foremost division in an expedition under General Forbes, which slowly cut its way through the rough wilderness of Pennsylvania, and, having at last got over the mountains, forced the French to leave Fort Duquesne. The fort was rebuilt by the English and renamed Fort Pitt, in honor of William Pitt, the great prime minister of

England, who was a true friend to the Americans. When a town grew around Fort Pitt it as called Pittsburg.

The war between the English and the French was finally closed in 1763. Canada, with all the country east of the Mississippi, was given up to the English, and settlers soon began to make their way into the region now known as Kentucky and Tennessee.

Before the war closed Washington retired to his home at Mount Vernon, and was married to Mrs. Martha Custis, a widow.

Washington in the Revolution

Washington lived for many years quietly at Mount Vernon, and he did not intend to have anything more to do with a soldier's life. He was fond of hunting and fishing. He sometimes helped to haul a seine in the Potomac River. He rode over his large plantation to see that all went well, and he made maps of all his fields, and kept his accounts carefully and neatly, as he had always done. All traveling strangers were sure of welcome at his house, and the poor, when in danger of suffering, were provided with corn from his granary.

But, as time went on, the English Parliament tried to collect a tax from the Americans. The Americans declared that, so long as they elected no members of Parliament, that body had no right to tax them without the consent. But the men who governed in England did not think that people in the colonies had the same rights as people in England, so they oppressed the Americans in many ways. Without asking consent of the colonies, they put a tax on all the tea that came into America; and when some of the tea got to Boston, the people turned Boston Harbor into one big teapot by pitching the whole shipload of tea into the water. The English government resolved to punish Boston, but the other colonies took sides with the people of that town.

In order to make the English government cease their oppressions, the Americans agreed not to wear clothes made of English cloth, nor to use anything else brought from England. Washington and other great gentlemen of that time put on homespun American clothes, which were coarse, for the Americans had not yet learned how to make fine goods. American ladies, who were extremely fond of tea, which they drank from pretty little cups brought from China, now gave up their favorite drink. Instead of it, they sipped a tea made from the leaves of the sage plants in their gardens, or from the roots and flowers of the sassafras. Probably they tried to drink these homegrown teas with cheerful faces, and to make believe that they liked sage and sassafras as well as the real tea from China. It must have been a pleasure to feel that they were fighting a battle for liberty over their tea tables.

Washington, in his quiet way, was a strong supporter of liberty against the King of England and the Parliament. In order to bring all the thirteen colonies to stand by one another against England a meeting, called a "Congress," was appointed in 1774, and men were sent from each colony to attend it. Washington was a member of this Congress, which sent a letter to the king, demanding that they should be allowed the same liberties as his subjects in England.

But neither the King of England nor the English Parliament would repeal the laws which the Americans disliked. As the Americans would not obey them, the quarrel grew hotter, and English troops were sent to bring the Americans to submit. On the 19th of April, 1775, the Revolutionary War was begun by a battle at Lexington, near Boston, between British troops and American farmers. These farmers, who were called "minutemen," drove the troops back into Boston, firing on them from every field and fence as they retreated.

Seeing that war had begun, Congress looked about for a leader. They remembered the prudent and brave conduct of Colonel George Washington, when a young man, in the French and Indian War. He was chosen to be general and commander in chief of all the armies of the colonies.

Before Washington reached the army near Boston, the battle of Bunker Hill had taken place. In this battle the Americans had been driven from the hill, but their little force of plain countrymen had fought so stubbornly against the well-trained English troops that all America was encouraged.

For many months Washington kept a fine British army shut up in Boston. When he was strong enough he suddenly sent a body of troops to Dorchester Heights, near Boston, where, by the help of bales of hay, breastworks were built in a single night. When the English general saw these works, he said, "The rebels have done more in one night than my army would have done in one month." The Americans began to throw shells from the Dorchester battery into Boston, which soon became so uncomfortable a place to stay in that the English army got into ships and sailed away.

The Americans at first were fighting only to get their rights as subjects of England. But since neither the King nor the Parliament of England would let them have their rights, they got tired of calling themselves Englishman. They determined to set up an independent government. On the 4th of July, 1776, Congress declared the colonies "free and independent." This is called the "Declaration of Independence."

Soon after the Declaration was adopted the English government sent a fleet and an army to take New York. Washington fought against the English army on Long Island, and was defeated and forced to give up New York. After a while he had to fall back across New Jersey. It seemed as though all were lost. But though his men were too few to fight the whole English army, Washington felt that he must strike a blow at some part of it in order to give the Americans courage. The English people did not like the war against the

Americans, so the king had hired some Hessian soldiers to fight for him. About a thousand of these were in Trenton, N.J., while Washington was on the other side of the Delaware, a little way off. On Christmas night the Hessians were celebrating the day. Washington celebrated it in his own fashion. He took part of his army, and crossed the Delaware in the midst of floating ice. There was a severe snowstorm, and two of his men were frozen to death. He marched quickly to Trenton, and after a sharp fight he took about a thousand prisoners, as Christmas presents for his country.

Washington got back across the Delaware with his prisoners, but in a few days he was again in Trenton, where he came near being surrounded and captured by the English general Cornwallis. The Delaware was so full of ice that the Americans could not get back to the other side of it, and a strong English force was pressing upon them in front. Something must be done quickly. So at night Washington had all his camp fires built up, in order to deceive the enemy. He put a few men to digging in the trenches, and had them make as much noise as possible. Then he took his army silently by a back road around the English army till he got behind it. While Cornwallis thought he had Washington cooped up in Trenton, the Americans were marching on Princeton, where there was a detachment of the English troops. Washington, after a sharp battle, defeated the English in Princeton. Cornwallis had gone to bed boasting that he "would bag the fox" in the morning; but when morning came, "the fox" was gone. Cornwallis thought at first that the Americans had retreated across the Delaware, but soon he heard the booming of cannons away behind him at Princeton; then he knew that Washington had outwitted him. He had to hasten back to New Brunswick to save his stores, while Washington went into the hills at Morristown, having forced the British to give up the greater part of New Jersey.

Seine, a long net for catching fish, which is dragged through the water by men pulling at each end of it. Gran'-a-ry, a building for storing grain. Parliament, the body of men which makes the laws of England, consisting of the House of Lords and the House of commons. Breast'-works, ridges of earth thrown up to protect an army in battle. Fleet, a number of ships of war under the command of one officer. Out-wit'-ted, defeated by greater ingenuity or cunning.

The Victory at Yorktown and Washington as President

In large histories you will read of the many battles of the Revolution, and of the sad sufferings of Washington's soldiers, who were sometimes obliged to march barefoot, leaving tracks of blood on the frozen ground. Sometimes a soldier had to sit be the fire all night for want of a blanket to cover himself with. There were not many people in this country then, and they were mostly farmers, with but little money. They were fighting against England, which was the riches and strongest nation of that time. But after a while France sent men and ships to help the United States to finish the war.

The Revolutionary War lasted about seven years in all. A great victory which Washington gained when the war had lasted more than six years really finished the struggle.

General Cornwallis, the same whom Washington had fooled when he slipped out of Trenton, had won several victories over American troops in the Southern States. But he could not subdue the people, who were always ready to rise up again when he thought he had conquered them. Cornwallis marched northward from Carolina into Virginia, where he did a great deal of damage. Washington was in the North watching New York, which was occupied by English troops. He thought if he could capture for fine army which Cornwallis commanded in Virginia he might end the war.

So, making every sign that he was going to attack New York, in order that soldiers might not be sent from New York to Cornwallis, he marched at the head of the American and French armies toward the South. On the way, he visited his home at Mount Vernon for the first time in six years.

Soon Cornwallis and his army were shut up in Yorktown, as Washington had once been shut up by Cornwallis in Trenton. But Cornwallis was not allowed to escape, as Washington did. Troops were sent all around him like a net, to keep him from getting away, while the French ships in Chesapeake Bay kept him from getting any help by way of the sea. The fighting about Yorktown was very severe, and the most splendid courage was shown by both the American and the French soldiers in charging the redoubts. The English fought with the greatest stubbornness on their side.

During the assaults Washington stood where he could see the bravery of the troops. One of his aids told him that it was a dangerous place for him to be in.

"If you think so you are at liberty to step back," said Washington.

Presently a musket ball struck a cannon near him and rolled at his feet. General Knox grasped Washington's arm, and said, "My dear general, we can not spare you yet."

"It is a spent ball. No harm is done," answered Washington.

Finding he could no longer resist, Cornwallis surrendered, and the war was virtually closed by the taking of Yorktown. The people of England had never liked this oppressive war, and the next year the English government felt obliged to acknowledge the independence of the United States.

Washington did not seek to make himself a king or a ruler over the country he had set free. When his work was over he gladly gave up command of the army, and went back to become, as he said, "a private citizen on the banks of the Potomac." While all the world was praising him, he went to work again taking care of his lands and crops at Mount Vernon, with the intention of never leaving his home for public life again.

But the people soon found that their government was not strong enough. Each State was almost a little country by itself, and the nation Washington and others had fought so hard to set free seemed about to fall into thirteen pieces. So a convention was called, to meet in Philadelphia in 1787, five years after the close of the Revolution. This convention, of which Washington was the president, made a new Constitution, which should bind all the States together into one country, under the rule of a President and Congress.

When the new Constitution had been adopted it became necessary to choose a President. Everybody wanted Washington to leave his fields and be the first President. He was elected by almost all of the votes cast.

At that time the capital of the country was New York. There were no railroads or telegraphs, so a messenger had to be sent from New York to Mount Vernon to tell General Washington that he had been chosen the first President of the United States. As the general traveled to New York the people turned out everywhere to do him honor. They rode by his carriage, and they welcomed him with public dinners in the towns. When he got to Trenton, out of which he had marched to escape from Cornwallis and fight the battle of Princeton, he found the bridge over which he had marched that night beautifully decorated. A triumphal arch had been erected by the women of Trenton, and, as the President passed beneath it, girls dressed in white sang a song of victory, and strewed flowers before him.

When he reached Elizabethtown Point there was in waiting for him a handsome large barge. In this he was rowed by thirteen master pilots dressed in white, and six other barges kept him company. The whole city of New York welcomed him with every possible honor. On the 30th of April, 1789, he took the oath of office, in the presence of a great throng of people.

Washington was again elected President in 1792. He refused to be elected a third time, and, after publishing a farewell address to the country, he left the presidency in 1797. He died at Mount Vernon in 1799.

Thomas Jefferson

Thomas Jefferson was the author of the Declaration of Independence. His father was a Virginia planter, and also a surveyor. The father was a man of strong frame, able to stand between two great hogsheads of tobacco lying on their sides and set both on end at once. He lived a hardy life, surveying in the woods.

Thomas Jefferson was born in 1743. His father died when he was fourteen, and left him the owner of a large plantation. Like most Virginia boys, he was fond of hunting, riding, and swimming. But he did not waste his life in sport. When he went to college at Williamsburg he became a famous student. Sometimes he studied fifteen hours a day, which would have been too much if he had not been strong. No man in all America, perhaps, was his superior in knowledge.

While he was a student, the colonies were thrown into violent excitement by the passage of the Stamp Act in England. This was a law for taxing the Americans, made without their consent. While this excitement was raging, young Jefferson went into the Virginia Legislature one day and heard the famous speech of Patrick Henry against the Stamp Act.

In the midst of his speech Patrick Henry cried out, "Caesar had his Brutus, Charles I his Cromwell, and George III," At this point everybody thought Henry was going to threaten the death of George III, who was King of England and of the colonies. This would have been treason. So, without waiting for Henry to finish, some of those who heard him broke into an uproar, crying out, "Treason! treason!" But when they paused, Patrick Henry finished by saying, "George III may profit by their example. If that be treason, make the most of it." This scene made a deep impression on young Jefferson.

Jefferson's wealth was in creased by his marriage. He build him a house which he called Monticello, meaning, "little mountain," from its situation on a high hill. Jefferson was very fond of trying new things. He introduced foreign plants and trees, and he bought in new articles of furniture and new ways of building houses.

While yet a young man he was sent to the Virginia Legislature, and then to Congress. He strongly favored the War of the Revolution. John Adams and others tried to persuade Congress to declare the colonies independent of England. At last a committee was appointed to write the Declaration. Jefferson was not a great speaker, but he was a brilliant writer. He wrote the

Declaration of Independence, and it was signed by the members of Congress on the Fourth of July, 1776.

In the Declaration Jefferson had declared that "all men are created equal." He now set about abolishing some of the laws which kept men from being equal in this country. In his own State of Virginia much of the land was tied up so that it could only descend to the oldest son. This was called the law of entail. Jefferson got this law abolished, so that a father's land would be more equally divided among his children.

There were also laws in most of the States which established some religious denomination as the religion of the State, and supported it by taxed. Jefferson got Virginia to pass a law separation the State from the Church, and making all men equal in regard to their religion.

Jefferson was governor of Virginia during part of the Revolutionary War, and he had to make great exertions to defend the State from the British. The British troops at length marched on Monticello, and Jefferson had to flee from his house.

Two of Jefferson's negro slaves, whose names were Martin and Caesar, made haste to hide their master's silver plate. They had raised a plank in the floor, and Caesar was crouched under the floor hiding the silverware as Martin handed it down to him. Just as the last piece went down, Martin saw the redcoats approaching. He dropped the plank, leaving Caesar a prisoner. In this uncomfortable place the faithful fellow lay still for three days and nights without food.

Jefferson was very loving and tender to his family. It was a great sorrow to him that four out of his six children died very young. His wife also died at the close of the Revolutionary War.

Jefferson was sent to take Franklin's place as American Minister to France. He was there five years, and then returned to America. He had always been kind to the negroes on his plantation. When he got back they were so rejoiced that they took him out of his carriage and carried him into the house, some of them crying and others laughing with delight because "massa come home again."

While Jefferson was gone, the Constitution of the United States had been adopted and General Washington had been elected President. He appointed Jefferson Secretary of State. Jefferson resigned this office after some years, and went back to Monticello.

In 1796 he was elected Vice President, and in 1800 he was chosen President of the United States. As President he introduced a more simple way of living and transacting business. He was much opposed to pomp and ceremony. It is said that when he was inaugurated he rode to the Capitol on horseback and hitched his horse to the fence. Another account has it that he walked there in company with a few gentlemen. At any rate, he would have no display, but lived like a simple citizen.

When Jefferson became President the United States extended only to the Mississippi River. President Jefferson bought from France a great region west of the Mississippi, larger than all the United States had been before that time. This is known as the "Louisiana purchase," because all the country bought from France was then called Louisiana. It has been cut up into many States since its purchase.

Jefferson was elected President a second time in 1804. In 1809 he retired to Monticello, where he lived the remainder of his life.

He was once riding with his grandson when a negro bowed to them. Jefferson returned the bow, but the boy did not. Jefferson turned to his grandson and said, "Do you allow a poor negro to be more of a gentleman than you are?"

While he was President, Jefferson was once riding on horseback with some friends. An old man stood by a stream waiting to get across without wetting his feet. After most of the others had passed over, he asked Jefferson to take him on behind and carry him across, which he did. When he had got down, a gentleman, coming up behind, asked him, "Why did you ask him, and not some other gentleman in the party?"

"I did not like to ask them," said the old man; "but the old gentleman there looked like he would do it, and so I asked him." He was very much surprised to learn that it was the President who had carried him over.

After Jefferson retired from the presidency so many people desired to see him that his plantation house was overrun with company, until he was made poor by entertaining those who came. It is related that one woman even poked a pane of glass out with her parasol, in order to see the man who wrote the great Declaration.

John Adams, the second President, and Jefferson, the third, lived to be very old. They died on the same day. Curiously, that day was the 4th of July, 1826. If you subtract 1776 from 1826, you will find that they died exactly fifty years after the day on which the great Declaration was signed. And they were the two men who had the largest share in the making of the Declaration of Independence.

Daniel Boone

Daniel boone was born in Pennsylvania in 1735. Boone was a hunter from the time he was old enough to hold a gun to his shoulder. He got just enough education to know how to read and write in a rough way. But in the woods he learned the lessons that made him the great pioneer and explorer.

One day the boy did not return from his hunting. The neighbors searched several days before they found him. He had built a little cabin of sod and boughs. Skins of animals were drying around the hut, and the young half-savage was toasting a piece of meat before the fire. This love for the wilderness was the ruling passion of his life.

By the time Daniel was thirteen the part of Pennsylvania in which he lived had become settled. The Boones, like true backwoodsmen, moved to a wilder region on the Yadkin River, in North Carolina. While Daniel's father and brothers cleared a new farm, the boy hunter was left to supply the table with meat.

One of Boone's modes of hunting was by "shining deer," as it was called in that country-that is, hunting deer at night with torches, and killing them by shooting at their glistening eyes. One night, Boone, hunting in this fashion, saw a pair of eyes shining in the dark which he thought to be deer's eyes, but which proved to be those of a neighbor's daughter, whom Boone afterwards married.

As the country was settling, he moved on to the headwaters of the river, where he and his young wife set up their log cabin in the lonesome wilderness. At this time the Alleghany Mountains formed a great wall, beyond which was a vast wilderness, with no inhabitants but Indians and wild animals. Boone was too fond of wild life and too daring not to wish to take on the other side. Fifteen years before the Revolutionary War began, he pushed across the mountain wall and hunted bears in what is now Tennessee.

In 1769 he went into Kentucky with five others. Here he hunted the buffalo for the first time, and came near being run down by a herd of them. At length he and a man named Stewart were taken captive by the Indians. Boone pretended to be very cheerful. When he had been seven days in captivity, the Indians, having eaten a hearty supper, all fell into a sound sleep. Boone sat up. One of the Indians moved. Boone lay down again. After a while he rose up once more. As the Indians all lay still, he wakened Stewart, and they took two guns and quietly slipped away, getting back in safety to a cabin they had built. But they never found any trace of the four men who had crossed the Alleghanies with them.

One day, when Boone and Stewart were hunting, a lot of arrows were shot out of a canebrake near them, and Stewart fell dead. Boone's brother and another man had come from North Carolina to find Daniel. The other man walked out one day and was eaten up by wolves. There were now only the two Boones left of eight men in all who had crossed the mountains.

By this time Boone ought to have had enough of the wilderness. But the fearless Daniel sent his brother back to North Carolina for ammunition and horses, while he spent the winter in this almost boundless forest, with no neighbors but Indians, wolves, and other wild creatures. This was just what Daniel Boone liked, for he was himself a wild man.

Once the Indians chased him. Seeing them at a distance, following his tracks like dogs after a deer, he caught hold of one of those long, wild grapevines that dangle from the tall trees in Kentucky, and swung himself away out in the air and then dropped down. When the Indians came to the place they could not follow his tracks, and Boone got away.

He lived alone three months, till his brother returned. Then the Boones selected a spot on which to settle, and went back to North Carolina for their families and their friends. On their way out again, in 1773, the Indians attacked Boone's party and killed six men, among whom was Boone's eldest son. The women of the party now went to the nearest settlement, but Boone made several journeys to and fro. In 1775, just as the Revolutionary War broke out, he built a fort in Kentucky, and called it Boonesborough. Even while building the fort Boone and his friends were attacked by Indians. When the fort was completed, Boone's wife and daughters came to Boonesborough, and they were the first white women in Kentucky.

A daughter of Boone's and two other girls were captured by the Indians while picking flowers outside of the fort. These cunning backwoods girls managed to drop shreds torn from their clothes, and to break a bough now and then, so as to guide their fathers in following them. The party was overtaken by Boone and others, and the girls were rescued.

To tell of all the battles around Boonesborough, or of all of Daniel Boone's fights and escapes, would take a great part of this book. Once, when hunting, he encountered two Indians. He "treed," as they called it-that is, he got behind one of the large trees of the forest. The Indians did the same. Boone partly exposed himself, and one of the Indian fired, but Boone, who was very quick, dodged at the flash of the Indian's gun. He played the same trick on the other. Then he shot one of the Indians, and killed the Indian with a knife such as hunters of that time carried in their belts.

One day Boone was attacked by a hundred savages. He tried the speed of his legs, but one young Indian was swifter than he, and he was captured. The Indians thought him a great prize. They shaved his head, leaving a single lock, painted his face, and dressed him up like an Indian. Then they gave him to an old woman who had lost her son. She had her choice to adopt him or give him up to be burned alive. After looking at him a long time the squaw made up her mind to adopt him.

The Indians among whom Boone was a prisoner were fighting on the English side in the Revolution. The English officers who were then at Detroit bought all their captives from the Indians, except Boone, and they offered five hundred dollars for Captain Boone. But the Indians would not sell so great a warrior. The English officers were sorry for him, and out of real kindness, when they could not buy him, they offered him money. Boone refused to receive any favors from those who were fighting against his country.

He pretended to like the Indian way of living. He stayed a long time with them, and took part in all their sports. He seemed to have forgotten his own people. But when he found that they were preparing to attack Boonesborough, he got ready to escape. Pretending to chase a deer, while holding a piece of his breakfast in his hand, he succeeded in getting away. By running in streams of water he kept the Indians from following his tracks. He lived on roots and berries, and only once ventured to discharge his gun to get food.

When he got back to Boonesborough he found that his family had given him up for dead and gone back to North Carolina. He repaired the fort, and beat off five hundred Indians who attacked it.

Boone brought his family to Kentucky again, and was in many severe fights after this. Kentucky had no rest from bloodshed until Wayne defeated the Indians in Ohio, in 1794. When Kentucky had filled up with people, the old pioneer went off to Missouri so as to get "elbowroom." The amusements of his old age were lying in wait for deer, shooting wild turkeys, and hunting for bee trees. He was eighty-five years old when he died.

Robert Fulton and the Steamboat.

More than a hundred years ago a sickly Scotch boy named James Watt used to sit and watch the lid of his mother's teakettle as it rose and fell while the water was boiling, and wonder about the power of steam, which caused this rattling motion. In his day there were no steamboats, or steam mills, or railways. There was nothing but a clumsy steam engine, that could work slowly an up and down pump to take water out of mines. This had been invented sixty years before. Watt became a maker of mathematical instruments. He was once called to repair one of these wheezy, old-fashioned pumping engines. He went to work to improve it, and he became the real inventor of the first steam engine that was good for all sorts of work that the world wants done.

When once steam was put to work, men said, "Why not make it run a boat?" One English inventor tried to run his boat by making the engine push through the water a thing somewhat like a duck's foot. An American named Rumsey moved his boat by forcing a stream of water through it, drawing it in at the bow and pushing it out at the stern. But this pump boat failed.

Then came John Fitch. He was an ingenious, poor fellow, who had knocked about in the world making buttons out of old brass kettles, and mending guns. He had been a soldier in the Revolution and a captive among the Indians. At length he made a steamboat. He did not imitate the duck's foot or the steam pump, but like most other inventors, he borrowed from what had been used. He made his engine drive a number of oars, so as to paddle the boat forward. His boat was tried on the Delaware River in 1787. The engine was feeble, and the boat ran but slowly. Fitch grew extremely poor and ragged, but he used to say that, when "Johnny Fitch" should be forgotten, steamboats would run up the rivers and across the sea. This made the people laugh, for they thought him what we call "a crank."

Robert Fulton was born in Pennsylvania in 1765. He was the son of an Irish tailor. He was not fond of books, but he was ingenious. He made pencils for his own use out of lead, and he made rockets for his own Fourth of July celebration.

With some other boys he used to go fishing on an old flatboat. But he got tired of pushing the thing along with poles, so he contrived some paddle wheels to turn with cranks, something like those in the picture. He was fourteen years old when he made this invention.

At seventeen he became a miniature painter in Philadelphia, and by the time he was twenty-one he had earned money enough to buy a little farm for his mother. He then went to Europe to study art.

But his mind turned to mechanical inventions, of which he now made several. Among other things, he contrived a little boat to run under water and blow up war vessels; but, though he could supply this boat with air, he could not get it to run swiftly.

He now formed a partnership with Chancellor Livingston, the American Minister to France, who was very much interested in steamboats. Fulton had two plans. One was to use paddles in a new way; the other was to use the paddle wheel, such as he had made when he was a boy. He found the wheels better than paddles.

He built his first steamboat on the River Seine, near Paris, but the boat broke in two from the weight of her machinery. His next boat made a trial trip in sight of a great crowd pf Parisians. She ran slowly, but Fulton felt sure that he knew just what was needed to make the next one run faster.

Fulton and Livingston both returned to America. Fulton ordered from James Watt a new engine, to be made according to his own plans. In August, 1807, Fulton's new boat, the Clermont, was finished at New York. People felt no more confidence in it than we do now in a flying machine. They called it "Fulton's Folly." How- ever, a great many people gathered to see the trial trip and laugh at Fulton and his failure. The crowd was struck with wonder at seeing the black smoke rushing from the pipes, and the revolving paddle wheels, which were uncovered, as you see in the picture, throwing spray into the air, while the boat moved without spreading her sails. At last a steamboat had been made that would run at a fair rate of speed.

The Clermont began to make regular trips from New York to Albany. When the men on the river sloops first saw this creature of fire and smoke coming near them in the night, and heard the puff of her steam, the clank of her machinery, and the splash of her wheels, they were frightened. Some of the sailors ran below to escape the monster, some fell on their knees and prayed, while others hurried ashore.

While Fulton was inventing and building steamboats, people became very much interested in machinery. A man named Redheffer pretended to have invented a perpetual-motion machine, which, once started, would go of itself. People paid a dollar apiece to see the wonder, and learned men who saw it could not account for its motion. Fulton was aware that it must be a humbug, because he knew that there could be no such thing as a machine that would run of itself. But his friends coaxed him to go to see it. When Fulton had listened to it awhile he found that it ran in an irregular way, faster and then slower, and then faster and slower again.

"This is a crank motion," he said. "If you people will help me, I'll show you the cheat."

The crowd agreed to help. Fulton knocked down some little strips of wood, and found a string running through one of them from the machine to the wall; he followed this through the upper floor until he came to a back garret. In this sat a wretched old man, who wore an immense beard, and appeared to have been long imprisoned. He was gnawing a crust of bread, and turning a crank which as connected with the machinery by the string. When the crowd got back to the machine room Redheffer had run away.

Fulton died in 1815. Before his death many steamboats were in use. Some years after his death steam was applied to railways, and a little later steamers were built to cross the ocean.

William Henry Harrison

One of the members of Congress who signed the Declaration of Independence in 1776 was Benjamin Harrison, a stout and jolly man. When Congress chose John Hancock for its President, or chairman, Hancock made a modest speech, as though he would decline the place. But Benjamin Harrison just took him up in his arms and set him down in the chair.

The third son of this Benjamin Harrison was William Henry Harrison. He was born in Virginia in 1773. His father died when he was young. Young Harrison began the study of medicine, but there was a war with the Indians in the West, and he wanted to go to the war. His guardian wished him to stick to his study of medicine; but there was more soldier than doctor in Harrison, and President Washington, who had been his father's friend, made the young man an officer in the army when he was but nineteen years old.

When Harrison got to the western country the army, under the lead of General St. Clair, had been surprised by the Indians and defeated. Washington appointed General Wayne to take St. Clair's place, and Wayne gave Harrison a place on his staff. Wayne trained his men carefully, and practiced them in shooting, and when he marched it was with every care not to be surprised. The Indians called Wayne "the Chief who never Sleeps." He fought a battle with the Indians on the Maumee River, in Ohio, and he pushed them so hotly with bayonets and guns fired at short range that the Indians fled in every direction. They were so thoroughly beaten that they made peace with the white people, and the Western settlers had rest from war for a while.

In 1801 a new Territory, called Indiana, was formed. It took in all the country which now lies in Indiana, Illinois, and Wisconsin, and it had but few white people in it. Harrison was made governor of this large region.

There was a young Shawnee warrior, Tecumseh, who had fought against Wayne in 1794. He was much opposed to the Indians' selling their lands. He declared that no tribe had a right to sell land without the consent of the other tribes. There were at that time seventeen States, and the Indians called the United States the "Seventeen Fires." Tecumseh got the notion of forming all the Indian tribes into a confederacy like the "Seventeen Fires," or States, of the white men.

Tecumseh was not born a chief, but he had gathered a great band of followers, and had thus become a powerful leader. He made long journeys to the North and West, and then traveled away to the South to bring the Indians into his plan for a great war that should drive the white people back across the Alleghany Mountains. In one council at the South the Indians refused to join him. Tecumseh told them that, when he got to Detroit, he would stamp on the ground and make the houses in their village fall down. It happened soon after that an earthquake did destroy some of their houses, and the frightened Indians said, "Tecumseh has arrived at Detroit." They immediately got ready to help him against the white people.

Tecumseh had a brother who pretended to be a prophet, and who was called "The Open Door." He gathered many Indians about him at Tippecanoe, in Indiana, and he preached a war against the white people.

Governor Harrison held a council with Tecumseh at Vincennes. Seats were placed for the chief on the piazza of the governor's house, but Tecumseh insisted on holding the council in a grove. He said that the white people might bring out some chairs for themselves, but that the earth was the Indians' mother, and they would rest on her bosom.

In the discussions Tecumseh grew very angry, and his warriors seized their tomahawks and sprang to their feet. Harrison drew his sword, a white man near him showed a dirk, and a friendly Indian cocked his pistol to defend the governor, while a Methodist minister ran with a gun to protect Harrison's family. Others present armed themselves with clubs and brickbats. The soldiers now came running up to fire on the Indians; but Harrison stopped them, and told Tecumseh that he was a bad man, and that he could now go.

Tecumseh cooled down and had another talk with the governor the next day, and Harrison even went to the chief's tent with only one companion.

But General Harrison soon saw that, in spite of all he could do, war would come. Tecumseh went South to stir up the Southern tribes. He gave these far-away Indians bundles of sticks painted red. He told them to throw away one stick every day, and, when all were gone, they were to fall upon the white people.

But General Harrison thought, if there had to be war, he would rather fix the time for it himself; so, while Tecumseh was leaving his almanac of red sticks in the South, the general marched from Vincennes, up the Wabash to Tippecanoe, which was Tecumseh's home. Knowing that the Indians would try to surprise him, he fooled them into believing that he was going up on one side of the river, and then crossed to the other. He got nearly to Tippecanoe in safety, but the prophet sent messengers to him, pretending that the Indians would make peace the next day.

Harrison's men lay on their arms that night. About four o'clock on the morning of November 7, 1811, the general was pulling on his boots, intending to awaken the army, when a sentinel fired at a skulking Indian, and the war whoop sounded from the tall grass on every side. The white men put out their camp fires, so that the Indians could not see to shoot at them, and the fierce battle raged in the darkness. The signals to charge and to fall back were given to the Indians by the rattle of deers' hoofs. The prophet sung a wild war song on the neighboring hill, after promising his followers that bullets should not hurt them. But many an Indian and many a white man fell in that bloody struggle. When daylight came, Harrison's men made a charge which drove away the savages.

Harrison burned the village of Tippecanoe, and Tecumseh came back to find his plan for driving the white men over the mountains spoiled. But the war with England broke out soon after this, and Tecumseh entered the British army, and was made a brigadier general.

General Harrison was now once more opposed to Tecumseh, for he was put in command of the United States army in the West. In 1813 he was besieged in Fort Meigs by an English army under General Proctor and a body of Indians under Tecumseh.

While the English were building their batteries to fire into the fort, the Americans were very busy also, but they kept a row of tents standing to hide what they were doing. When the English guns were ready, the Americans took down their tents and showed a great earthwork that would shelter them from the batteries. This made Tecumseh angry. He said that General Harrison was like a ground hog—he stayed in his hole, and would not come out and fight like a man.

Proctor, though belonging to a civilized nation, was a heartless brute. Tecumseh was a born a savage, but he was always opposed to cruelty. Some of Harrison's men had been captured, and Proctor allowed the Indians to put them to death. When Tecumseh saw what was going on, he rushed in between the Indians and their prisoners with his tomahawk in hand, and stopped the slaughter.

"Why did you allow this?" he demanded of General Proctor.

"I could not control the Indians," said Proctor.

"Go home and put on petticoats," said Tecumseh.

The English fleet on Lake Erie was beaten in a fight with the American ships under Commodore Perry in the fall of 1813. Harrison now crossed into Canada, and the British army retreated to the river Thames, where Harrison overtook it, and a battle followed. Proctor was afraid to fall into the hands of the Americans, who hated him for his cruelties to prisoners and the wounded. He ran away before the battle was over. Brave Tecumseh was killed in this fight.

Harrison left the army soon after this. In 1840 he was living in a simple way on his farm at North Bend, in Ohio, when he was nominated for President of the United States. He was elected, but he died on the 4th of April, 1841, one month after taking office.

Andrew Jackson

General Andrew Jackson's father was also named Andrew Jackson. He was an Irishman, who came to the Waxhaw settlement, on the line between North and South Caroline, about ten years before the Revolution. He had built a log cabin, cleared a little land, and raised a crop of corn, when he sickened and died. In this sad time his son, Andrew Jackson, was born. Andrew's mother lived with her relatives, and spun flax to earn a little money.

From a little fellow "Andy" was a hot-tempered boy. Some larger boys once loaded a gun very heavily, and gave it to Andy to fire, in order to see him knocked over by the "kick" of the gun. But the fierce little fellow had no sooner tumbled over, than he got up and vowed that he would kill the first one that laughed, and not one of the boys dared to provoke him. He grew up in a wild country and among rough people. What little schooling he got was at an old-field schoolhouse.

When he was but thirteen the Revolutionary War began. In the South the struggle was very bitter, neighbor battling against neighbor with any weapons that could be found. Of course, a fiery fellow like Andrew wanted to have a hand in the fight against England. Whenever he went to a blacksmith's shop he hammered out some new weapon. Young as he was, he was in two or three skirmishes. In one of these, Andrew and his brother were taken prisoners. A British officer ordered Andrew to clean the mud off his boots. Young Jackson refused, and got a sword cut on his head for it. His brother was treated in the same way. The two wounded boys were then confined in a forlorn prison pen, where they took the smallpox. Their mother managed to get them exchanged, and brought the sick boys home.

When Andrew Jackson was eighteen years old he went to the village of Salisbury to study law. At this time many settlers were crossing the mountains into the rich lands to the westward, and young Jackson moved to the newly settled country of Tennessee. Here, in the fierce disputes of a new country, it took a great deal of courage to practice law.

Jackson was not only brave; he was also a quick-tempered man, who got into many quarrels during his life, and sometimes fought duels. The rough people among whom he lived were afraid of him. One day he was eating at a long table which the keeper of the tavern had set out of doors for the crowd that had come to see a horse race. A fight was going on at the other end of the table; but fights were so common in this new country that Jackson did not stop eating to find out what it was about. Presently he heard that a friend of his, one Patten Anderson, was likely to be killed. Jackson could not easily get to his friend for the crowd, but he jumped up on the table and ran along on it, putting his hand into his pocket as though to draw a pistol. He cried out at the same time, "I'm coming, Patten!" and he opened and shut the tobacco box in his pocket with a sound like the cocking of a pistol. The crowd was so afraid of him that they scattered at once, crying "Don't fire!"

Jackson was an able man, and an honest one in his way. He was once a judge, he kept a store, he went to Congress, and then to the United States Senate. When the "War of 1812" with England broke out he was sent as a general of Tennessee volunteers to defend New Orleans. When he had waited some time at Natchez he was ordered to disband his troops, as they were not needed. Those who sent such an order from Washington did not stop to ask how the poor Tennesseeans were to make their way back to their homes. Jackson refused to obey the order, pledged his own property to get food for his men, and marched them to Tennessee again. The men became devoted to him, and gave him the nickname of "Old Hickory."

But after a while war broke out in the Southwest in earnest. Tecumseh, in his Southern trip, had persuaded a half-breed chief, who was known to the whites as Weathersford and to the Indians as Red Eagle, to "take up the hatchet" and go to war. The Indians attacked Fort Mimms, in which four hundred men, women, and children were shut up. They burned the fort and killed the people in it. Weathersford tried to stop the massacre, but he could not control his savages.

When the news of this slaughter reached Tennessee Jackson was very ill from a wound in the arm and a ball in the shoulder which he got in a foolish fight. But in spite of his wounds, the fiery general marched at the head of twenty-five hundred men to attack the savages. He had a great deal of trouble to feed his troops in the wilderness; the men suffered from hunger, and some times rebelled and resolved to go home. Jackson once ordered out half his army to keep the other half from leaving. Again, the half that had tried to desert was used to make the others stay. At another time he stood in the road in front of his rebellious soldiers, and declared in the most dreadful words that he would shoot the first villain who took a step.

In spite of all these troubles with his wild soldiers, Jackson beat the enemy by rapid marches and bold attacks. In 1814 the savages had fortified themselves at a place called Horseshoe Bend. Here Jackson had a terrible battle with the Indians, who fought until they were almost all dead. At length most of the savages submitted, or fled into Florida, which at that time belonged to Spain. The white men had vowed to kill Weathersford, the chief; but that fearless fellow rode up to Jackson's tent, and said that he wanted the general to send for the Indian women and children, who were starving in the woods. When the white soldiers saw Weathersford, they cried out, "Kill him!" But Jackson told them that anybody who would kill so brave a man would rob the dead.

Jackson was suffering all this time from a painful illness, and was hardly able to sit in the saddle. But he marched to Mobile, which he succeeded in defending against an English force that had landed in Florida, and had been joined by Florida Indians. Jackson resolved that the Spaniards should not give any further aid to the enemies of the United States. He therefore marched his army into Florida and took the Spanish town of Pensacola, driving the English away.

It soon became necessary for him to go to New Orleans to defend that place. The English landed twelve thousand fine men below that city. Jackson armed the free negroes and the prisoners out of the jails, but, after all, he had only half as many soldiers as the English. The general, though yellow with illness, was as resolute as ever. He had several fights with the English as they advanced, but the decisive battle was fought on the 8th of January, 1815, when the English tried to carry the American works by storm. Jackson's Southwestern troops were many of them dead shots. They mowed down the ranks of the British whenever they charged, until more than one fifth of the English troops had been killed or wounded and their general was also dead. Though the English had lost twenty-six hundred brave men, the Americans had but eight killed and thirteen wounded.

One little English bugler, fourteen years old, had climbed into a tree near the American works and blown his bugle charge, to cheer the English, till there were non left to blow for. An American soldier then brought him into camp, where the men made much of their young prisoner, because he was so brave.

This wonderful defense of New Orleans ended the "War of 1812." General Jackson became the darling of his country. When the United States bought Florida from Spain, he was sent to take possession of that country.

In 1828 Jackson was elected President of the United States. He was a man of the plain people, rough in speech and stern in manner, but his popularity was very great. He was the first President who put out of office those who had voted against him, and appointed his own friends to their places. He enforced the laws with a strong hand, and he managed affairs with other nations in such a way as to make the country respected in Europe.

General Jackson died in 1845. He was, as we have seen, a man of strong will and fierce passions. But he was faithful to his friends, affectionate with his relatives, and exceedingly kind to his slaves. He had no children, but he adopted a nephew of his wife and brought him up as his son. He also adopted an Indian baby, found after one of his battles in its dead mother's arms. His splendid defense of New Orleans showed Jackson to be one of the very ablest generals American has ever produced.

Morse and the Telegraph

Before the railroad and the telegraph were invented it took weeks for news to go from one part of this country to another. The mails were carried by a lad on horseback, or by a stagecoach drawn by horses. The railroad was invented in England and introduced into this country about 1830. The locomotive carried news much more quickly than horses' feet could travel. But now we know to-day what happened yesterday on the other side of the world, and we wonder how people ever got on without the electric telegraph.

Samuel Finley Breeze Morse, who invented the electric telegraph, or that form of it that came into general use, was born in Charlestown, Massachusetts, in 1791. When he was four years old he was sent to school to an old lady, who was lame and not able to leave her chair. She managed her scholars with a very long rattan stick. This was her telegraph, we might say, but the children did not always like the messages she sent upon it. Morse showed his talent as an artist by scratching a picture of the old lady on a piece of furniture, but he did not like the message she sent him on her rattan telegraph.

When Samuel Morse went to Yale College he took great interest in the experiments in electricity which he saw there. But the chief question with him at this time was how to get a living. He had a talent for making pictures, and he took to painting miniatures of people for five dollars apiece; he also made profiles at a dollar apiece. As there were no photographs then, people who wanted small pictures of themselves had to have them painted. This was usually done on ivory.

We have seen that Fulton, the maker of steamboats, was a painter. Morse became a painter, and went to England to study, where he attracted attention by his good work. After four years in Europe he came to America again, as poor as ever. His clothes were threadbare, and his shoes were ragged at the toes. "My stockings," he said, "want to see my mother." He brought with him a large picture, which everybody admired, but nobody bought it.

He was already thinking about inventions. He and his brother invented a pump, which his brother jokingly named "Morse's Patent Metallic, Double-headed, Ocean-drinker and Deluge-spouter Valve Pump Box." But the pump, for all this, was not a success, and Morse traveled from town to town painting portraits for a living.

Morse went to Europe again, and in 1832 he sailed for America once more. He was now about forty-one years old. One evening, in the cabin of the ship, the talk turned on electricity. A Dr. Jackson, who was one of the passengers, told of an interesting experiment which he had seen in Paris. Electricity had been sent instantaneously through a great length of wire arranged in circles around a large room.

"Then," said Morse, "I don't see why messages can not be sent a long distance instantaneously by means of electricity."

When the conversation was over the rest forgot all about it. But Morse began to plan a telegraph, making drawings of the machine in his sketch-book. But he was much too poor to go on with his invention. His brothers gave him the use of a room for a studio, and here he lived, and made experiments on a rude telegraph. He did his own cooking, and he used to go out at night to buy food, for fear that his friends should discover how little he had to eat.

In 1835 Morse became a professor. He now took a Professor Gale into partnership in the telegraph. But neither of them had money enough to perfect the invention. While they were one day exhibiting their rude machine to some gentlemen, a student named Alfred Vail happened to come into the room. Young Vail was the son of Judge Vail, a wealthy mill owner. He had worked for some years in his father's shops, and was a far better mechanic than Professor Morse or Professor Gale.

Vail's quick eye soon comprehended the new invention, which was being tested with seventeen hundred feet of wire stretched back and forth across the room.

"Do you intend to try the telegraph on a large scale?" Vail asked.

"I do, if I can get the money to carry out my plans," Professor Morse replied.

Vail then proposed to get money for Morse if the professor would make him a partner. This was agreed to, and the young man hurried to his room, locked the door, threw himself on his bed, and gave himself up to imagining the future of the telegraph. He took up his atlas and traced out the great lines which the telegraph would take. It is probable that Professor Morse would have failed if it had not been for the help of this young man.

After getting some further explanations from Morse, Alfred Vail hurried home and talked to his father about it until the judge decided to furnish the two thousand dollars that would be needed to make a perfect telegraph. This was to be taken to Congress, to persuade that body to supply money to build the first line.

Besides furnishing money for the machine, the Vails got Morse to paint some portraits for them, and thus supplied him with money to meet his most pressing wants. Alfred now had a room fitted up in one of his father's workshops at Speedwell, in New Jersey. He kept the place carefully locked, lest the secret of the invention should be discovered by others.

A boy named William Baxter, fifteen years old, was taken from the shop to help Alfred Vail. For many months Alfred and Baxter worked together, sometimes day and night. There was no such thing as telegraph wire in a day when there were no telegraphs. But the ladies of that time wore a kind of high bonnet, which was called a "sky-scraper," and a sort of wire was used to strengthen and stiffen the fronts of such bonnets, which proved to be the best to be had for the purpose of the new telegraph makers. Vail bought all the bonnet wire in the market.

Vail made many improvements in Morse's machine. He also made the instrument write, not with the zigzag marks used by Professor Morse, but in dots and dashes for letters. Morse was busy getting his patent, and Professor Gale was engaged in making the batteries.

How the Telegraph Became Successful

Morse now had but three pupils. One of his pupils, when his quarter's tuition was due, had not yet received his money from home, so that he could not pay the professor immediately. One day, when Morse came in, he said:

"Well, Strother, my boy, how are we off for money?"

"Professor, I'm sorry to say I have been disappointed, but I expect the money next week."

"Next week!" exclaimed Morse; "I shall be dead by next week."

"Dead, sir?"

"Yes, dead of starvation."

"Would ten dollars be of any service?" asked Strother, in alarm.

"Ten dollars would save my life; that is all it would do," answered the professor, who had not eaten a mouthful for twenty-four hours. The money was paid.

Judge Vail grew discouraged about the telegraph. The old gentleman refused to look at the machine. Alfred Vail saw that if the work were not finished soon his father would put a stop to it. He and young Baxter stayed close in their room, with Morse, working as fast as they could, and avoiding Judge Vail, lest he should say the words that would end their project. Baxter would watch the windows, and, when he saw Judge Vail go to dinner, he would tell Morse and Alfred Vail, and they would all go to dinner at the house of Alfred's brother-in-law, making sure to get safe back before the judge should appear again.

At last the invention was in working order, and Alfred Vail said to Baxter:

"William, go up to the house and ask father to come down and see the telegraph machine work."

The boy ran eagerly, in his shop clothes and without any coat, and Judge Vail followed him back to the little room. Mr. Vail wrote on a slip of paper, "A patient waiter is no loser." He handed this to Alfred, saying:

"If you can send that so that Professor Morse can read it at the other end of the wire, I shall be convinced."

Alfred clicked it off, and Morse read it at his end. The old gentleman was overjoyed.

But there was a great deal of trouble after this in getting the matter started. It was thought necessary to have the government build the first line, because business men were slow to try new things in that day. The President, and other public men, showed much curiosity about the new machine, but Congress was slow to give money to construct a line.

In 1842 a bill was passed in the House of Representatives appropriating thirty thousand dollars to construct a telegraph on Morse's plan from Washington to Baltimore. It had yet to pass the Senate before it could become a law. When the last hours of the session had arrived, a senator told Morse that his bill could not be passed, there were so many other bills to be voted on before it. Morse went to his hotel, and found that, after paying his bill and buying his ticket to New York, he had thirty-seven cents left.

But the next morning, while he was eating his breakfast before leaving Washington, Miss Ellsworth, the daughter of the commissioner of patents, brought Morse word that his bill had passed the night before. For her kindness the inventor promised her that she should send the first message over a telegraph line.

Morse tried to lay his wires underground in pipes, but it was found that naked wires laid in this way let the electricity escape into the ground. What was to be done? There were now but seven thousand dollars left of the thirty thousand. To change their plan would be to confess that those who were building the telegraph had made a mistake, and this would make people more suspicious than ever. The machine for digging the ditch in which the wires were to be laid was run against a stone and broken on purpose to make an excuse for changing the plan.

A year had been wasted, when it was decided to put the wires on poles. At last, in 1844, the wires were strung, and Miss Ellsworth sent the first message, which was, "What hath God wrought!" The first news that went over the wire was that James K. Polk had been nominated for President.

But at first people would not believe that messages had come over the wire. They waited for the mails to bring the same news before they could believe it. One man asked how large a bundle could be sent over the wires. A joking fellow hung a pair of dirty boots on the wire, and gave it out that they had got muddy from traveling so fast. A woman who saw a telegraph pole planted in front of her door said she supposed she could not punish her children any more without everybody knowing it. She thought the wire would carry news of its own accord. At first few messages were sent. The operators worked for nothing, and slept under their tables. But after a while people began to use the wires, which were gradually extended over the country. Another kind of electric telegraph had been tried in England, but Morse's plan was found the best.

Before Morse put up his first line he had tried a telegraph through the water. To keep the electricity from escaping, he wound the wire with thread soaked in pitch and surrounded it with rubber. He laid this wire from Castle Garden, at the lower end of New York city, across to Governor's Island, in the harbor. He was able to telegraph through it, but before he could exhibit it the anchor of a vessel drew up the wire, and the sailors carried off part of it.

About 1850, Cyrus W. Field, of New York, got the notion that a telegraph could be laid across the Atlantic Ocean. After much thought to raise the money needed, and two attempts to lay a telegraph cable across the ocean, the first cable was laid successfully in 1858. The Queen of England sent a message to the President of the United States, and President Buchanan sent a reply. Many great meetings were held to rejoice over this union of the Old World with the New. But the first Atlantic telegraph cable worked feebly for three weeks, and then ceased to work altogether.

Mr. Field now found it hard work to get people to put money into a new cable. Seven years after the first one was laid, the Great Eastern, the largest ship afloat, laid twelve hundred miles of telegraph cable in the Atlantic Ocean, when the cable suddenly broke. The next year, in 1866, the end of this cable was found and brought up from the bottom of the sea. It was spliced to a new one, which was laid successfully.

Morse lived to old age, no longer pinched for money, and honored in Europe and America for his great invention. He died in 1872, when nearly eighty-one years old.

The latest wonder in telegraphing is the telephone, which is a machine by which the actual words spoken are carried upon a wire and heard at the other end of the line. The invention was made about the same time, in somewhat different forms, by several different men.

Early Life of Abraham Lincoln

Five years after Daniel Boone took his family to Kentucky there came over the mountains a man named Abraham Lincoln, bringing his wife and children. The Lincolns and Boones were friends. They were much the same kind of people, hunters and pioneers, always seeking a new and wild country to live in. This Abraham Lincoln, the friend of Boone, was a grandfather of President Abraham Lincoln, who was born in a log cabin in Kentucky in 1809.

When little Abe Lincoln was seven years old, his father moved from Kentucky to southwestern Indiana, which was then a wild country. Here he lived in a house of the roughest and poorest sort known to backwoods people. It had three sides closed with logs. The other side was left entirely open to the weather. There was no chimney, but the fire was built out of doors in front of the open side. There was no floor. Such a wretched shelter is called a "half-faced camp." It is not so good as some Indian wigwams. Of course, the food and clothes and beds of a family living in this way were miserable.

Poor little Abe Lincoln sometimes attended backwoods schools. The log schoolhouses in Indiana at that time had large open fireplaces, in which there was a great blazing fire in the winter. The boys of the school had to chop and bring in the wood for this fire. The floor of such a schoolhouse was of rough boards hewn out with axes. The schoolmasters were generally harsh men, who persuaded their pupils to study by means of long beech switches, such as they were accustomed to use in driving oxen. These schoolmasters did not know much themselves, but bright little Abe Lincoln soon learned to write. This was very handy for his father and other men in the neighborhood who could not write, and who got Abraham to write their letter for them.

Lincoln could not get many books to read in a community so destitute and illiterate. He could not have wasted his time and weakened his mind, as so many boys and girls do now, by reading exciting stories, for he did hot have them. He read carefully the books that he had. The Bible, Æsop's Fables, Pilgrim's Progress, a life of Washington, and life of Henry Clay he read over and over again, for he could get no other books. Whenever he heard any subject talked about that he did not understand, he would go off alone and think it out, and try to put it into clear words. This habit of close and careful thinking, and this practice in clothing his thoughts in word that exactly fitted them, was the best education in the world. Many boys and girls who have good schools and good books never learn to think for themselves.

When one is poor, a little money means a great deal. One day Abraham Lincoln, by this time eighteen years old, rowed two men with their baggage from the shore out to a steamboat in the Ohio River. For this the men dropped two silver half-dollars into the boat. Abraham was overjoyed. To think that a poor boy could earn so much money in so short a time made the whole world seem wider and fairer before him, he said.

The people of southern Indiana in that day used to send what they raised on their farms to New Orleans. They loaded their corn, hay, and potatoes on large flatboats, sometimes a hundred feet long. These boats were floated on the current of the Ohio River to where that river empties into the Mississippi, and then down the Mississippi. It was a long voyage, and the boatmen had to live on their boats for many weeks. They rowed the boats with long sweeps, or oars, which required two and sometimes four men to move each one of them. Lincoln was much trusted, and when he was nineteen years old he was sent down the river in charge of one of these boats. This gave him his first knowledge of the world.

By the time he was twenty-one he had attained the height of six feet four inches. His father, who was always poor, once more sought a newer country by removing to Illinois. Here Abraham helped to build a log cabin, and then he split the rails to make a fence around the new cornfield. In order to get clothes, he went out to work as a hired man on a neighbor's farm. The cloth used by the Western people at that time was woven by hand in their own homes. Lincoln had to split four hundred rails to pay for each yard of the homespun brown jeans that went to make his trousers. Perhaps he was sorry to be so tall and to need so much cloth for a pair of trousers.

Lincoln went a second time on a flatboat to New Orleans. The boat was loaded with live hogs, and it is said that Lincoln, finding that the hogs could not be driven, carried them on board that boat in his long arms. After he came back he became a clerk in a country store, where he employed his spare time in reading. Like Franklin, he got his education by the right use of his leisure time. In this store he showed that careful honesty for which he was always remarkable. Once, when by mistake he had taken a "fip"—that is, six and a quarter cents—more than was due from a customer, he walked several miles the same night to return the money. When he found that, by using the wrong weight, he had given a woman two ounces of tea less than she ought to have had, he again walked a ling distance in order to make the matter right.

One of the things he wanted to learn was English grammar, in order to speak more correctly; but grammars were hard to find at that time. He heard of a man eight miles away who had a grammar, so he walked the eight miles and borrowed it. Lincoln got a lawyer who sometimes visited the store to explain what he could not understand in his grammar.

Lincoln in Public Life

In 1832, when there was an Indian war in Illinois, known as the Blackhawk War, Lincoln volunteered to fight against the chief Blackhawk and his Indians. Lincoln was chosen captain of the company. But he did not happen to be in any battle during the war. He used to say, jokingly, that he "fought, bled, and came away."

When "Captain" Lincoln got home from the Blackhawk War, he bought a country store in New Salem, when he lived. He had a worthless young man for a partner, and Lincoln himself was a better student than merchant. Many bad debts were made, and, after a while, as Lincoln expressed it, the store "winked out." This failure left him in debt. For six years afterwards he lived very savingly, until he had paid every cent of his debts. After he ceased to keep store he was postmaster. In a country post office he could borrow and read his neighbor's papers before they were called for. He used to carry letters about in the crown of his hat, and distribute the mail in that way.

Next he became a surveyor. He studied surveying alone, as he did other things. His strict honesty and his charming good-nature, as well as his bright speeches, amusing stories, and witty sayings, made him a favorite among the people. In 1834 he was elected to the Illinois Legislature. In a suit of homespun he walked a hundred miles to attend the Legislature. When the session was over he came home and went to surveying again. Whenever he had a little money he applied himself to studying law. When his money gave out he took up his compass and went back to surveying.

In 1837 he went to Springfield, and began life as a lawyer. The lawyers of that day rode from county to county to attend the courts. Lincoln "rode the circuit," as it was called, with the others, and he was soon a successful lawyer. He would not take a case which would put him on the unjust side of a quarrel. Nor would he take pay from people whom he knew to be poor, so he did not become a rich man.

Lincoln was always remarkable for his kindness of heart. While riding along the road one day he saw a pig fast in a mudhole. As he had on a new suit of clothes he did not like to touch the muddy pig, and so he rode on, leaving piggy to get out if he could. But he could not get the pig out of his thoughts, so, when he had gone two miles, he turned his horse back and helped the floundering pig out of his distress. He said he did this to "take a pain out of his own mind."

Once a poor widow, who had been kind to him many years before, asked him to defend her son, who was on trial for murder. It was proved in court by a witness that in a drunken row this widow's son had struck the blow that killed the man. Everybody thought the young man would be hanged. When questioned by Lincoln, the witness said that he had seen the murder by moonlight. Then Lincoln took a little almanac out of his pocket, and showed the court that at the time the man was killed the moon had not risen. The young man was declared "not guilty," but Lincoln would not take any pay from the mother.

In 1846 Abraham Lincoln was elected a member of Congress. This was during the war with Mexico. In that day the Southern States allowed negroes to be held as slaves. The Northern States had abolished slavery, so that part of the States were called free States and part slave States. There came up, about this time, a great debate as to whether slavery should be allowed in the new Territories. Lincoln strongly opposed the holding of slaves in the Territories, and he soon became known as a speaker on that side of the question. His fame reached to the East, and Abraham Lincoln, who had come up from the poverty of a half-faced camp, was invited to address a large meeting in the great hall of Cooper Institute, in New York. You see, the boy who had tried to think everything out clearly, and to put every subject into just the right words, had got such a knack of saying things well, that multitudes of educated people were delighted to listen to his clear and witty speeches.

When, in 1860, the antislavery men came to nominate a President, many of the Western people wanted Lincoln, whom they had come to call "Old Abe," and "Honest Old Abe." When the convention that was to nominate a President met, the friends of Lincoln carried in two of the fence rails he had split when he was a young man, and thousands of people cheered them. Lincoln was nominated, and, as the other party split into two parts, he was elected.

This election was followed by the great civil war. The war made President Lincoln's place a very trying one, for people blamed him for all defeats and failures. But during all the four years of war he was patient and kindly, and by his honesty and wisdom he won the affections of the people and the soldiers. People thought of him at first as only a man who had happened to get elected President. But during these long years he showed himself a great man, and when the war was ended he was respected over all the world.

When the terrible war was over and the soldiers were coming home, Lincoln was shot by an assassin as he sat in the theater, on the 14th of April, 1865. His death was lamented not only over all this country, but throughout Europe, for his goodness of heart made him as much loved as his greatness of mind made him admired.

Something About the Great Civil War

Soon after Abraham Lincoln became President there broke out the civil war, which caused the death of many hundreds of thousands of brave men, and brought sorrow to nearly every home in the United States. Perhaps none of those who study this book will ever see so sad a time. But it was also a brave time, when men gave their lives for the cause they believed to be right. Women, in those days, suffered in patience the loss of their husbands and sons, and very many of them went to nurse the wounded, or toiled at home to gather supplies of nourishing food for sick solders in hospitals.

The war came about in this way: There had been almost from the foundation of the Government a rivalry between the Northern and Southern States. Long and angry debates took place about slavery, about the rights of the States and the government of the Territories. These had produced much bitter feeling. When a President opposed to slavery was elected, some of the Southern States asserted that they had a right to withdraw from the Union. This the Northern states denied, declaring that the Union could not be divided; but before Lincoln was inaugurated, seven States had declared themselves out of the Union. They formed a new government, which they called "the Confederate States of America," and elected Jefferson Davis President.

President Lincoln refused to acknowledge that the Confederate States were a government. He refused to allow that United States fort in the harbor of Charleston, South Carolina, to be surrendered to the Confederates, and he sent ships with provisions for the small garrison of this fort. The Southern troops about Charleston refused to let these provisions be landed, and at length opened fire on the fort. This began the war. Four other States now joined the Confederacy, making eleven in all.

It was a time of awful excitement in every part of the country. All winter long angry passions had been rising both in the North and in the South. When the first gun was fired at Sumter, in April, 1861, there was such a storm for fierce excitement as may never be seen again in America. In the North, a hundred thousand men were enlisted in three days. The excitement in the South was just as great, and a large portion of the Southern people rushed to arms. In those stormy times the drums were beating all day long in the streets; flags waved in every direction, and trains were thronged with armed men bidding farewell to friends and hastening forward to barrel and death. Men and women wept in the streets as they cheered "the boys" who were hurrying away to the war. For a while people hardly took time to sleep.

We can not tell the story of the war in this book; you will study it in larger histories. The armies on both sides became very large, and during the war there were some of the greatest conflicts ever seen in the world. The first great battle was fought at Shiloh, in Tennessee. Others took place at Murfreesboro, Chickamauga, and Nashville, in Tennessee; at Antietam, in Maryland; and at Gettysburg, in Pennsylvania. Very many battles, great and small, were fought in Virginia, between Washington and Richmond.

On the side of the Union the three most famous generals were U. S. Grant, W. T. Sherman, and Philip H. Sheridan. The three greatest generals on the Confederate side were Robert E. Lee, Joseph E. Johnston, and Thomas J. Jackson, commonly called "Stonewall Jackson."

Both sides showed the greatest courage. The generals on both sides were very skillful. Victory was now with one party and now with the other; but, as the years passed on, the Union armies, being the stronger, gradually gained one advantage after another. By means of troops and gunboats sent down from the North under Grant, and a fleet under Admiral Farragut, which was sent around by sea to capture New Orleans, the whole of the Mississippi River was secured. Between Washington and Richmond the Confederates won many victories, but they were at length compelled to fall back behind the fortifications of Richmond and Petersburg, where they were besieged by General Grant.

During the time of this siege General Sherman marched directly into the heart of the Confederacy, where he was for weeks without any communication with the North. He marched across the great and fertile State of Georgia, from Atlanta to Savannah, on the seacoast, and then from Savannah northward toward Richmond. By destroying the railroads and the food by which General Lee's army in Richmond was supplied, this march of Sherman's made it impossible for the Confederates to continue the war.

Lee was forced to retreat from Richmond, and he surrendered his army on the 9th of April, 1865. All the other Confederate forces soon after laid down their arms. The war had lasted four years. As a result of the long struggle, slavery was abolished in all the territory of the United States.

Something about the Spanish War

The war with Spain took place in 1898. It was caused by two things. For many years there had been a rebellion against Spain in Cuba. Our people were very sorry for the Cuban people, who were treated cruelly. This made the Spaniard angry at the United States. One of our war ships, the Maine, was sent to the harbor of Havana, to protect Americans there. It was blown up in the night and two hundred and sixty-six men on board were killed. An examination showed that it was blown up by something placed against the outside of the ship. This aroused the American people. Congress demanded that Spain should take her armies away from Cuba. This she refused to do, and war was declared.

When war was declared, there was an American fleet in Chinese waters. There was a Spanish fleet at Manila in the Philippine Islands, which belonged to Spain. Commodore Dewey, who commanded the American fleet, sailed to Manila as soon as he heard of the beginning of the war.

Not finding the Spanish fleet outside of the harbor, he sailed into the great Bay of Manila very silently. This was about midnight before the morning of the first day of May. All the lights on the ships that could have been seen from the shore were put out, so that the last ship was passing the batteries at the entrance to the bay before the alarm was given. At daylight the ships gave battle to the Spanish fleet, which was protected by shore batteries. It seemed certain that some, if not all, of the American ships would be sunk by the heavy guns on shore, but the Spanish gunners were not equal to those of the American ships, who had given much attention to target practice. The Spaniards fought bravely, but their shore batteries were silenced and their fleet destroyed by the American fire. The American fleet did not lose a single man in the fight.

A Spanish fleet sent from Spain to attack the American coast towns took refuge in the harbor of Santiago in Cuba. The harbor was so well protected that the American fleet could not enter it. An army was landed to the east of the city of Santiago to take it by land. One portion of this army was sent to take the little village of El Caney at the north, and another was sent to wait in front of the hill of San Juan and capture that after El Caney was taken. But the men in front of the batteries of San Juan found themselves under fire. Many of them were killed. They could not retreat, for the narrow road behind them was crowded. They were not willing to stay where they were and be slaughtered. So they resolved about noon to attack the Spaniards in the batteries ahead of them. "If you don't wish to go along," said the colonel of the regiment known as the Rough Riders, "let my men pass, please." But the men to whom he spoke did wish to go along. They fell into line and followed Roosevelt, who led a desperate charge on horseback. In another part of the line a veteran general, Hawkins, rode at the head of his men, waving his hat. Slowly up the hill marched the Americans under a deadly fire, until at last they carried the trenches and blockhouse at the summit with a rush.

Three miles away, at El Caney, a yet more stubborn fight was raging. The Americans in the thick of it were commanded by General Chaffee, who made his men lie down but who stood erect himself. A button was shot off his coat, and one of his shoulder straps was torn by bullets. At last the works at El Caney were carried. These battles took place on the 1st of July.

Two days after the battles by which the Americans carried the Spanish trenches, the American ships were watching the mouth of the harbor as usual. To their surprise the Spanish fleet was seen coming out from Santiago. The Spanish ships tried to escape by running to the westward. But the American ships pursued and fought them until one after another of the Spanish vessels was sunk or set on fire. The American sailors rescued as many as possible of the drowning Spaniards, and treated them kindly. The city of Santiago was soon after surrendered. After these successes of the Americans it was impossible for Spain to continue her resistance long. Peace was made at last. As a result of the war Spain gave up her authority over Cuba, Porto Rico, and the Philippine Islands.

How The United States Became Larger

When Washington was a young man, the French claimed all the land west of the Alleghany Mountains. If the French had succeeded in holding all this western country the United States would always have been only a little strip of thirteen States along the Atlantic coast, reaching from Maine to Georgia. But by conquering Canada the English got possession of all the territory east of the Mississippi River. This was given up to England by the French in the treaty made twelve years before the Revolutionary War. Daniel Boone and other settlers soon afterwards crossed the mountains and began to take possession of the great West.

During the first year of the Revolution no care was taken to drive the British from the forts in the West. But in 1778 George Rogers Clark led a little band of Kentucky settlers through the wilderness to the Mississippi River, where he captured the British fort at Kaskaskia, in what is now Illinois. He then marched eastward and captured Vincennes, in the present State of Indiana. These and other victories of Clark gave the United States, at the close of the war, a claim to all the country lying east of the Mississippi.

In 1803, twenty-one years after the close of the Revolutionary War, President Jefferson bought from France all that large region beyond the Mississippi River known then as Louisiana. It has since been cut up into many States and Territories. The size of the country was more than doubled when Louisiana was added to it.

The province of Louisiana did not reach to the westward of the Rocky Mountains. But in 1791, before Louisiana was bought, Robert Gray, the first sea captain that ever carried the American flag around the world, discovered the river Oregon, which he called the Columbia, after the name of his ship. After Jefferson had bought Louisiana for the United States, he sent the explorers Lewis and Clark with a party to examine the western part of the new territory, and to push on to the Pacific. These men were two years and four months making the trip from St. Louis to the Pacific Ocean and back. They reached the ocean in 1805, and spent the winter at the mouth of the Columbia River. The "Oregon country," as it was called, was then an unclaimed wilderness, and the discovery of the river by Captain Gray, with the exploration of the country by Lewis and Clark, gave the United States a claim to it. The peninsula of Florida was occupied by the Spaniards more than forty years before the first colony of English people landed at Jamestown.

From the time the colonies were settled, there were many quarrels between the people of this country and the Spanish inhabitants of Florida. But in 1821 Florida was bough from Spain, and became a part of the United States.

Mexico, which was at first a Spanish colony, rebelled against Spain, and secured its independence. One of the States of the Mexican Republic was Texas. Americans who had settled in Texas got into a dispute with the government of Mexico. This took the form of a revolution, and Texas became an independent republic, under a president of its own. In 1845 this republic of Texas was annexed to the United States by its own consent, and has been from that time the largest State in the Union.

The Mexicans, though driven out of Texas, were quite unwilling to lose so large a territory. The annexation of Texas to the United States led to a war with Mexico, which lasted two years. During this war the United States troops took from Mexico California, on the Pacific coast, and a large region known as New Mexico, in the interior. At the close of the war, in 1847, this territory was retained by the United States, which paid to Mexico fifteen million dollars for it. Another small tract was bought from Mexico in 1851, which we may account part of the addition from Mexico in consequence of the war, and consider the two together.

Made in the USA
Lexington, KY
24 July 2017